For Isaac
I hope you enjoy this ___.
His life is very inspirational
and what's exciting is that he
earned two degrees from Oberlin

The Sword and the Broom

The exceptional career and
accomplishments of
John Mercer Langston

College where I met your grandparents.
I enjoyed learning more about
Oberlin while researching his story.

Linda Salisbury

Your grandparents are special
friends from our student days
together.

Happy birthday!
Linda Salisbury

Tabby House

Contents

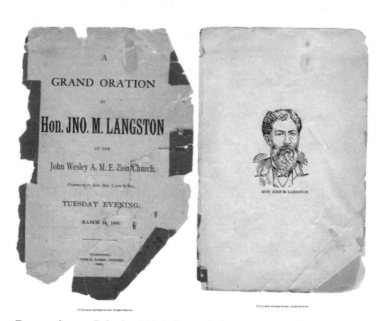

Pages from John's 1891 Grand Oration on the status of blacks. (Courtesy of the Historically Black College and University Library Alliance and Virginia State University Archives.)

Introduction

I WAS INSPIRED TO "RETELL" John Mercer Langston's autobiography for a new audience after reading his 534-page original, visiting the remains (before planned restoration) of his father's plantation home in Louisa, Virginia, and because we share a common bond as graduates of Oberlin College. His story is one of self-reliance triumphing over adversity; of knowing the importance of education, and of fighting for the rights of all under the Constitution. He was a proud American, who dedicated his life to the welfare of black citizens and service to his country.

He was a man of many state and national firsts for black Americans: first attorney in Ohio; first elected official; first admitted to practice before the Supreme Court, and first to represent Virginia in the United States Congress. He helped rewrite state constitutions after the Civil War, and to draft a Civil Rights bill. He also founded and served as dean of Howard University's law school, and was the first president of what is now Virginia State University. He was the inspector general of the Freedmen's Bureau, and was appointed as what's now called "ambassador" to Haiti.

Yet few people, even Virginians, know his name (unlike the older, celebrated Frederick Douglass).

Unable to find a modern version for young adults, I have written a "retelling," closely following his autobiography *From the Virginia Plantation to the National Capital, or the First and Only Negro Representative in Congress from the Old Dominion* as my guide. I selected stories and events that I felt were most compelling and relevant.

Acknowledging that some terms in common use during his lifetime are no longer preferred, I have changed "colored" and "Negro" in most instances to "black." ("African-American" was not widely used until the 1980s.) I have not repeated the n-word, although he quoted it in disparaging remarks made about himself and others.

Langston's autobiography was curiously written in the third person, perhaps to imply objectivity about reporting his numerous accolades and praise. His book is less reflective than episodic. My retelling remains episodic to be faithful to his version.

His time lines can be confusing, creating awkward progressions in the narrative, particularly when he writes about moving to the farm in Brownhelm, and marrying Caroline. These events should overlap (a month after he moved to the farm, they married and soon lived there), but he doesn't mention their marriage and her arrival until pages later with implication that he was initially alone on the farm with his tenants. I decided to follow his flow rather than attempt to rewrite these sections, except for moving his stories of family illnesses in Haiti from the end of the book to the Haiti chapter.

There are frustrating gaps in personal information, such as what happened to his brothers after he was dropped off with the Gooch family (both Gideon and Charles enrolled at Oberlin). Did his family move with him to various locations when he changed jobs? I believe that his omissions were deliberate—to separate his professional career and accomplishments from his personal life.

Perhaps in the haste of writing, and without modern research tools (the Internet for fact-checking) Langston has occasional incorrect spellings of names (Governor "Todd," and Professor "Shurtliff") which I've corrected. I've also searched out missing details where possible, such as his contemporaries' full names, and their roles during those periods in American history. I think he may have assumed that his readers knew about the events and people that he mentions.

Wherever possible I've included verbatim language, dialogue and dramatic moments—when he was naughty in school, or is denied admission to law school. I think readers will cheer his measured but forceful confrontation with the law school's owner. I've added conversation and small details, such as

7

what might have been in his shiny new lunch bucket to enliven his stories.

Besides studying his autobiography, I've read a number of documents about him, communicated with members of historical societies, visited Virginia sites where he would have been, and searched the digital archives of Oberlin College, Virginia State University, the Library of Congress, the National Archives and other sources. I've read his speeches, the minutes from his contested election, and books and articles. (I was surprised at how much written about him is not correct, i.e., he was never a slave.)

This doesn't make me an historian, only someone deeply curious, and eager to share Langston's life story.

Cerebral and scholarly, Langston reveals emotion—when he is orphaned for a second time; when he flubs his first oratory at Oberlin; and when he must leave his family in Oberlin to answer his country's call to help the newly freed. His frustration and justifiable bitterness with the political system that fraudulently denied him his congressional seat for almost his entire term seeps into his lengthy account of the election of 1888.

He was a highly principled man, who argued against the evils of slavery, and that the Declaration of Independence and the Constitution applied to all people. That was his fight.

Readers may be surprised to learn about his rivalry with Douglass, most evident during

Langston's congressional campaign. Douglass' attack was personal and it obviously angered and hurt Langston. His autobiography was likely an attempt to set the record straight for his legacy. William Cheek's article (see resources, page 199) on the election of 1888 provides other details on their animosity and public perceptions.

I chose *The Sword and the Broom* (see chapter 15) as the title because these images represent Langston's triumph over the enemies who denied him his congressional seat. He did not give up despite obstacles.

Another story of breaking down barriers is not found in the narrative, but was told by his great-nephew, the famed poet Langston Hughes. Hughes relates that when his namesake was serving in Congress, he was barred from riding in his elegant carriage pulled by two white horses through a white neighborhood near the Capitol. Langston ordered his coachman to stop, handed him his gloves, and with an axe chopped down the barricades so that they could drive on down the road. There were no more problems.

Issues of race and racism, unfortunately, continue to be part of the national fabric and conversations, making this courageous and remarkable man's narrative even more relevant, especially when we observe the 2016 election season at state and national levels.

Through this retelling, I hope I have done justice to Langston's inspiring life story.

Time Line

1829 December 14, born in Louisa County, Virginia

1844–49 Attends Oberlin College, Ohio; graduates with honors.

1852 Receives master's degree in theology from Oberlin Theological Seminary

1854 Admitted to the Ohio Bar

1854 Marries Caroline M. Wall

1855 October 25, Elected clerk of Brownhelm Township in Ohio.

1856 Elected to the city council of Oberlin, Ohio

1860–1871 Elected member of the Board of Education of Oberlin, Ohio

1863 Recruiter of colored soldiers for the 54th and 55th Massachusetts Regiments and the 5th Ohio.

1867 Appointed General Inspector of the Freedmen's Bureau; admitted to practice law before the U.S. Supreme Court.

1868–1875 Dean of the Law Department of Howard University

1873–1875 Acting-president of Howard University.

1871 Sought by Senator Charles Sumner (Mass.) to help draft Civil Rights Bill

1871–1877 Appointed by President Grant to Board of Health of the District of Columbia.

1877–1885 Appointed by President Hayes as minister resident of Haiti and later, charge d'affaires to Santa Domingo

1885–1888 President of Virginia Normal and Collegiate Institute (now Virginia State University, Petersburg, Virginia)

1888 Runs for Congress from Virginia's Fourth District. Fraudulent election denied him his seat for nineteen months

1890 September 23, seated in the House of Representatives

1894 Publishes autobiography

1897 Dies, November 15

1

Louisa Orphan

ON A SWELTERING SUMMER DAY in 1834, little John Mercer Langston kicked a stone in the direction of the smokehouse, then found a sturdy stick that was strong enough for him to practice his letters in the hard, dry dirt. He squatted under the black cherry tree and spelled his mother's name, LUCY, just as his older brother Charles Henry, now sixteen, had taught him. Both Charles and Gideon, still older at twenty-four, had started their education with their father when they were seven. They had opened their books at five A.M. each day before they joined the plantation slaves to help with chores. Charles was happy to share what he had learned with his inquisitive little brother.

John begged his brothers to read to him and teach him to write his letters, but he had especially enjoyed sitting on his father's lap while the wealthy landowner read aloud from George Washington's *Rules of Civility and Decent Behavior.*

John and his father liked Number 16: "Do not Puff up the Cheeks." They immediately stared at each other with cheeks puffed fully until one or the other began laughing.

John tried to remember what the big words meant as he recited the rules back to his father. Sometimes they looked at maps or his father would read him scary stories about children who didn't listen to their elders.

"You're going to do well, John Mercer," his father said. "And when you're older, we'll start with real learning, just like your brothers did."

"When will I be seven, Father?" John asked one snowy day that winter.

"You were just four in December, so three more years. You're more than halfway there." His father tousled John's straight dark hair and bounced him on his knee.

But just as spring flowers were blooming in the fields, and the green shoots of wheat, corn and tobacco were popping up through the red soil, John's father, Ralph Quarles, became ill. The special orange poppies John picked to make his father smile no longer made the elderly man feel better. Ralph had died, and now John's mother, Lucy Jane Langston, was ill, too.

Lucky, one of the house slaves who loved John dearly and had been helping raise him since he was born, carried the small boy into Great House for his father's funeral. She also made sure now that he saw his mother each day while Lucy was awake and asked for him. John was about to spell out his own name with the stick when he heard Uncle Billy calling for him from near the barn.

"Come, Johnnie," he said. "I'm going to Kent's Mill with the wagon. Sacks are ready to be picked up."

John dropped the stick and ran past the house to where Uncle Billy was hitching the team of horses that were the coppery color of Virginia clay. Although small for his age—about three feet, eight inches tall—John was able to climb up into the wagon seat. With a flick of the reins, Uncle Billy, the oldest of the slaves, urged the horses into action and the wagon creaked behind them as they started down the dirt road to the mill. John hoped that Uncle Billy would tell him another ghost story to help take his mind off his mother, whose eyes were closed so much of the time.

The wagon had barely reached the narrow road when Uncle Billy said, "I've heard things in the night again. Strange noises, Johnnie."

"What kind of noises?" asked the boy, wiggling his dusty toes with delight.

"Ghosts that come by the cabins and Great House," said Uncle Billy.

"Ghosts came to your cabin?" asked John. "Weren't you scared?"

"Oh, yes," said Uncle Billy. "They moan, and beg for food and shelter."

"Ghosts don't eat food," said John. "Charles says ghosts don't eat anything because they're ghosts and you can see through them."

13

"Now what does Charles Henry know about ghosts here on this plantation?" said Uncle Billy, giving John a sideways glance.

John wasn't sure who was right. Charles said many times that Uncle Billy was superstitious but John liked Uncle Billy's stories anyway. They sounded true. "What did you feed the ghost?"

Uncle Billy replied, "First I have to tell you what he looked like. He was wild and mysterious. A big black man with long hair and a beard. He pounded on the door of your father's house. Even though he was frightened, Burrel opened the door, and the big man said, 'Boys, I've come for something to eat!' He scared a lot of people but he has friends here and all around."

"Friends?"

"Yes, his friends are people like us. We help him, but don't you talk about it," said Uncle Billy. "The ghosts are fugitive slaves. They're on the run and hiding until they're safe."

John puzzled over this. "They're not real ghosts?"

Uncle Billy shook his head and ran his fingers through his gray hair. "They're ghosts because we pretend we don't see them. People that help them don't see them. They're running to freedom in places like Ohio."

"Are you a runaway slave, Uncle Billy?" John asked.

"No, John. There are slaves, including me, on this plantation to work the fields and help at the house. Your mama was a slave that your daddy set free along with your sister, Maria. He set others free, too. He was a good and fair man. I never needed to run away. I know I'm talking over your head but it's something I've got to say."

John didn't understand, but he knew that Uncle Billy sounded sad so he listened hard.

"Captain Quarles had a different system of running the plantation. He didn't have an overseer. Lots of those overseers on other places are mean— really cruel—to slaves. They whip and starve them, and slaves' families are sold apart from each other. Not right and people run away to get to freedom. Nobody should be a slave. Nobody."

He paused and glanced at John who looked a lot like his mother—small-built, light-skinned, dark hair and eyes. Uncle Billy, the oldest and most respected slave on the plantation, could remember when Captain Quarles, a Revolutionary War hero, had built the big white wooden house in Louisa County, Virginia, and had acquired Lucy from a man who owed him money. Ralph then emancipated Lucy, and their daughter, Maria, and made sure that both would always be free. Lucy also had three other children, William, Mary, and Harriet, who were freed. Then Ralph and Lucy had three sons together. All of her children would have her last name—Langston. Ralph and Lucy lived together, as if married, for almost thirty years.

In October 1833, six months before Ralph Quarles died, he signed a will leaving his land on Hickory Creek (more than 2,000 acres), cattle, money, and bank stock to his three sons and appointed trusted executors to take care of his wishes. He had already left other property to Lucy.

Uncle Billy shook his head about the laws that kept Ralph and Lucy from ever marrying. And there was still some danger for the boys because although they were mixed-race, they were considered black and therefore subject to laws regarding blacks. How could that be explained to anyone, even someone as young and smart as John? He would need to know all about these things too soon, Uncle Billy knew.

"So, John, I'm really glad that you and your brothers were born free," said Uncle Billy.

John had heard about being born free before, even though he didn't quite understand what it meant. He knew that his father was white and his mother was mostly Indian and black. Color didn't matter to him—his or anybody else's, whom he knew or played with. Gideon was as light-skinned as his father, and had added Quarles as his middle name. Charles was the darkest of the three boys, and John, very light (a "bright mulatto").

John wanted to hear more about the ghosts.

"What do you feed the ghosts?" he asked.

"Whatever we have to give," said Uncle Billy with a deep sigh. "And we pack food for them to take along the way through the mountains to safety in Ohio. Many runaways hide in these woods, but they aren't safe. We all have to help everyone be free. You must help, too, Johnnie."

Uncle Billy sounded so serious that John didn't think he should ask more about the ghosts. Besides, they were heading down the hill to his favorite creek, where he could wade in the cool water while Uncle Billy talked with the miller's slaves about the harvest and what was going on at Great House.

When they returned with sacks of cornmeal, John's nursemaid, Lucky, was waiting in the yard. Her face was streaked with tears. "John Mercer Langston, where have you been? You should have told me you were going off with Uncle Billy. Your mama needs you right away! She's been asking for you. She cried and said, 'Oh, that I could see my children once more.'"

Lucky didn't wait for John to answer, but lifted him off the wagon and raced to Lucy's house at the end of the garden. He wanted to say, "Put me down," but he didn't think she'd stop long enough. Lucky sat John on his mother's bed. Lucy's long dark hair that John loved to stroke, spilled onto her pillow. He felt Lucky's hands on his shoulders. "She has something to say to you, Johnnie."

John was now more scared than he had ever been. Something even worse than the day before and the day before that was going on. He could see shadows of other people in the room, standing back against the walls, watching him. The windows were open with a view to the rolling hills, the trees that still had their summer green, and crops of tomatoes, beans, and corn.

"Mama?" John said. "Mama, wake up. I didn't have time to pick you flowers. I'll go get some."

"John," whispered his mother, pulling him down on her where she could wipe his face and stroke his hair. "My baby. You can pick them later. Let me kiss you one more time." Her voice was soft. Too soft. "Remember how we've loved you. I know you'll make us proud."

She hugged him until her arms relaxed and Lucky lifted him off the bed and carried him out of the room. He could hear sobbing and wails that became so loud that his ears hurt.

It was 1834. John, not yet five, was an orphan.

When his father died, the family, the slaves and the freed mourned him privately for two days in the big house. After Lucy's funeral, Lucky carried little John to the site where his mother's grave was located under a tree next to his father's. Lucky soothed his aching heart as best she could and tried to comfort him. She wanted to tell him everything would be okay, but she knew what was going to happen. The plantation family would be separated; she would never see him again.

Later John sat on the front steps of Great House and listened to Gideon and Charles conversing with their father's friends and nephews. He was tired and what they were saying didn't make sense. There was talk about selling the plantation and moving to Ohio. He curled up on the step and fell asleep, awakened later by Charles Henry, who called for Lucky to take John to bed.

No one at the plantation had expected both parents to die within months of each other, even though Lucy had not been well for some time. Ralph had died at age seventy but Lucy was only fifty-four. What had been a family of families would now be family groups going their separate ways. Some would still live as slaves, given to relatives of Ralph Quarles, according to Ralph's will. Four slaves—Uncle Billy, Arthur, Burrel, James Jr.—would travel with John, Gideon, and Charles to Ohio, where they would live in freedom.

Ralph, a wealthy man, also wanted to ensure that his sons would inherit his money and property, and would be well educated. Lucy's will had provided for their daughter, Maria, now twenty-eight years old. Although he had owned slaves out of necessity,

Great House, built by Ralph Quarles, father of John Mercer Langston. The addition to the right is not original. A second house with basement-level kitchen in the rear is connected to the Great House. (author photo, 2016)

Stairs and doorways from the house above the Great House kitchen. (author photo)

Ralph felt slavery was wrong. He tried to do what was right for members of the plantation family. When Maria, "pretty, smart and well educated," fell in love with a slave named Joseph Powell, Ralph purchased Joseph and several other slaves to give to her. She and Joseph married and had twenty-one children.

Original smokehouse adjacent to Captain Quarles' plantation home outside Louisa Courthouse, Virginia. (author photo)

A small brick fireplace on the second floor of Great House. (author photo 2016)

In his will, Ralph named several friends to take care of his property and the welfare of his children. Colonel William Gooch and his family, who had recently moved to Chillicothe, Ohio, had agreed to serve as John's guardian if something happened to Ralph and Lucy.

In the days that followed Lucy's burial, John often wandered around Great House. Even though his father had died several months earlier and his mother had been sick and in bed for a long time, John still hoped to find them. Maybe if he went inside one last time before they left for Ohio they would be there and he wouldn't have to go away. But his father wasn't sitting by the fireplace in the parlor reading a book, and his mother wasn't in the brick kitchen under the smaller attached house. Her clothes were gone from her garden home. Someone had packed away quilts that had been stored in the sunny room above the kitchen. The room was empty. John climbed up the three tall steps and opened the small door in the wall then continued up the steps to the second floor where he sometimes played a hiding game with Lucky. He stood on his toes and looked out the window. Lawrence and Abram were removing slabs of pork from the smokehouse. Johnson and Ann were coming back from the barn carrying chickens in woven baskets. The trees beyond the field had changed to bright orange and gold. The slaves saw John peering out the window, his chin barely touching the sill, and waved.

John opened the door to the hall that crossed into Great House, wishing he would find his mother sitting in a rocker next to the small brick fireplace. She would be singing and mending his father's shirt. She would be happy to see him and would invite him to sit and maybe she'd tell him a story about her mother, who was a full-blooded Indian from the tribe related to Pocahontas. He wished he could remember his mother's songs, but he was having trouble remembering her face. He didn't mean to cry but silent tears spilled anyway.

When John came down the steps he saw that his brothers and the people who had taken care of the plantation were in the yard gathering their belongings to take to their new homes. Their sadness was as terrible as when his parents died. Whites and blacks embraced and wept as they said their farewells. Lucky rushed over and hugged little John.

"Aren't you coming?" John asked. He was frightened.

"No, baby child. We're going that way," she said pointing, "to a new place. You come back and see us someday," she said. "I'll always remember you."

"Who's going with you?" John asked.

"My granny and pappy, Jacob and Winney, my mama Lucy, and my sisters and brothers— Johnson, Martha, Anthony, Edward, Henry and Ann. Look over there. You can see them loading up."

John couldn't hold back a sob and then a wail, that joined with a chorus of grieving members of the plantation. Lucky dried his tears as her own fell. "You'll be fine, child. Look, here comes your brother."

Illustration found on page 30b of John's autobiography, From the Virginia Plantation to the Nation's Capitol, *titled "Leaving the Virginia Plantation."*

Charles said, "There you are, Johnnie. The wagons are packed. We've got our shoes and clothes, hats and food. Ready?"

John wanted to beg him to let Lucky come, but he heard Uncle Billy talking to Gideon about him.

"Are you sure John's up to traveling?" asked Uncle Billy. "He's so little and it's a long and tiring trip."

Uncle Bill added, "And, Gideon, do we have our papers to prove we are free?"

Gideon assured him that John would be all right. "And yes, I have the papers that show that Johnnie, Gideon and I are free, plus your emancipation papers. Here's the $220 that father wanted you to have to start a new life, and $120 each for the others."

Uncle Billy said, "Captain Ralph was a good man. Thank you."

With that, the brothers, plus the four soon-to-be-free slaves, boarded the two wagons and were on their way to Ohio with heavy hearts.

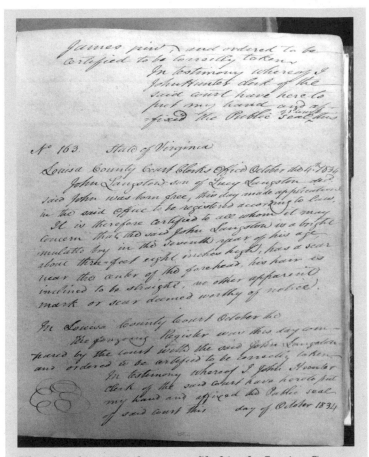

This October 1834 document filed in the Louisa County Courthouse registered John Mercer Langston a "bright mulatto, of three feet eight inches, with straight hair and a scar on his forehead," as a free person. All free blacks were required to register including John and his brothers. Although John's father was white, John was considered "Negro" due to his mother's black and Native-American heritage. Free blacks were required to carry a copy of their registration at all times in order to avoid captivity, especially when they traveled. (Courtesy of the Louisa County Historical Society.)

Linda Salisbury

Those who owned slaves or defended the system of slavery often based their argument on the need to have cheap labor to run their large farms, typically several thousand acres, primarily in Southern states. The types of farm machinery now available had not yet been invented and there weren't enough nonslaves to work the fields. Men, women and children were captured in Africa, the Caribbean, and even in the American colonies (Native Americans) and were sold at auctions. Families were divided, never to see members again. Because slaves were considered property to be bought and sold, when one ran away, the owner wanted to have his "property" returned to him. Runaway or fugitive slaves headed for freedom to states or areas that did not allow slavery, but that didn't stop slave-hunters from trying to catch them and return them to their owners. The underground railroad was a network of people who provided safe places for runaway or fugitives to hide and be helped, often with transportation to the next stop or station until they were safe in a free state, such as Ohio, parts of the Northeast or Canada. The Fugitive Slave Act of 1850 meant that runaways, and freed slaves alike, were not safe, even in states where slavery was illegal.

Little Johnnie Gooch

JOHN'S MEMORIES OF LEAVING Great House and the people they left behind faded as the wagons bumped and jiggled along the rocky roads across swollen rivers and rocky creeks that led to the Allegheny Mountains. His brothers entertained him with what they had heard about Ohio and from stories they had read. To keep him busy, Gideon told John to let him know what animals he spotted. John was most excited when he saw two bear cubs high in a tree.

At dusk, they would stop for the night, feed and water the teams of horses, and pitch their tents. They ate cold food: ham and chicken from the smokehouse, apples from the orchards, hard biscuits and eggs, and savored warm drinks of tea and coffee.

In the morning they made mush by stirring cornmeal into hot water before the wagons pressed on to the north and the west. The warm October days quickly turned frigid after sunset. Gideon made sure that John was well wrapped in blankets and warmed by the fire. As they neared the mountains, the brothers kept John bundled in extra layers of clothing, and pulled the cap that Lucky had made for him over his ears.

John leaned against Charles as they rode, and he wondered if Uncle Billy, who was driving the team, had seen ghosts in the woods when branches creaked and leaves rustled. He was afraid to ask.

On the third day, Gideon told John about the family he would be living with when they reached their new home. "Do you remember Colonel Gooch, Father's friend?"

"Not really," John replied.

"He's a wonderful man," said Gideon, "and you'll like him, and also his wife and three daughters. They'll probably spoil you. You wouldn't mind that a bit."

"Will they have slaves?" asked John. "Will Lucky be there?"

"No, not anymore," said Charles Henry. "No slavery in Ohio. It's a free state. And Lucky's still in Louisa, living on a different plantation with her family. Now, hang on, we're crossing another stream."

In the distance, John could see the high mountains. As the wagons drew closer, they looked even bigger. Almost a week had passed since they had left the plantation. While they made their camp for the night near a stream where they could water the horses, suddenly a man on horseback appeared. John was so startled that he clung to Uncle Billy's leg. He didn't know who the stranger was or what he wanted. John relaxed when he saw that Gideon and the others were warmly welcoming the fellow, with hugs and shouts of "glad you found us."

As they ate pieces of smoked ham and squash cooked over the fire, the man made everyone laugh with tales of his adventures. John had no trouble staying awake to listen to the stories about living in Ohio. He learned that this dark-skinned man had left Ohio on the same day that they had departed from Louisa because he wanted to meet them on their journey and to guide them. Nobody told John why. Who was he?

Finally, the man lifted John onto his lap and cuddled him saying, "You are the picture of your mother, John." And then he laughed and added, "And the image of your father." This had John puzzled until the man finally identified himself. He was John's half-brother, William Langston, who had been born to his mother, Lucy, before she gave birth to Gideon, Charles and John.

William was so excited to see John that on the next morning after the wagons were repacked, he insisted on adjusting the stirrups of his saddle to fit John's short legs and held him in front of him as they continued the journey.

"I never met you before," John said, as he happily settled into the saddle, with William's arms around him.

"That's because your good father freed us before you were born. Your half-sisters, Harriet and Mary and I moved to Ohio, where you're going now. I've been there ever since. My sisters don't like the cold weather in the North."

"What do you do?" asked John.

"I'm a carpenter and a joiner," said William. "I build things with wood. I'll teach you how someday. Everybody needs a trade and it pays well."

William talked nonstop, which made the journey more interesting. After two more weeks they crossed the Kanawa River by ferry, then came to the Ohio River and, then crossed to Gallipolis.

Instead of being happy, Uncle Billy and the others former slaves seemed worried about what might happen to them. Were they really free? They were nervous because people were looking at them funny after they crossed the river.

Gideon tried to reassure the men. "You've got your emancipation papers."

"I can't read what they say," confessed Arthur.

"Well, I know what they say, and father's word is good," Gideon said. "You are free."

It hadn't occurred to John that his friends from Virginia wouldn't be going all the way with him. He thought everyone would be staying with the Gooch family, his new home. But after about three days of travel in Ohio, they reached the black settlement of Berlin. Then Uncle Billy, Burrel, James Jr. and Arthur unpacked their possessions from the carry-all wagon and said good-bye. They would use the money from Captain Quarles to purchase land.

"Good-bye." John curled up in a ball to hide his tears.

Uncle Billy squatted next to the boy, lifted his face and looked him in the eyes. "John," he said, "You are going to do well wherever you go and I'll be thinking of you always. Now remember what I told you about taking care of the ghosts. I'm counting on you. We're all counting on you."

John nodded without understanding. "I promise."

Within two more days, the brothers reached Chillicothe. What a sight they were! Their horses were exhausted and skinny, and the wagon showed wear. The brothers were worn out, eager for good fresh food, and in need of baths and clean clothes.

As the horses clopped through the city streets, John's brown eyes widened with amazement. He'd never seen a place like this. It was so much bigger and grander than the town of Louisa, which he had visited when his father had business at the courthouse.

"Soon we'll be at the Gooches' farm on the other side of town. It's right on the Ohio Canal. You'll get to see boats go by, and maybe go fishing, John Mercer," said Gideon.

"And we've heard that lots of folks from Louisa live here now," said Charles. "They'll want news from home."

While Charles and Gideon made temporary arrangements at a boarding house for themselves and the horses, William continued on the path along the canal to deliver John to the Gooch family.

John gripped the armrest of the wagon as they neared a large stone house. He was a bit apprehensive.

"That's where you'll be living," said William. "Don't worry. We'll all be looking out for you."

The stone house was not at all like Great House or the other Louisa plantation homes that were typically constructed of wood and painted white. The Gooches' large place in Virginia, called Ben Lomond, had been made of wood and brick.

The wagon stopped near the front door and Colonel Gooch rushed out to greet John. The boy who had been worried only moments earlier about what his new family would be like was immediately happy. After seeing Colonel Gooch's friendly face and big blue eyes, John knew he could trust him. Mrs. Gooch hurried out behind the colonel. She was small, like John's mother Lucy. Matilda Gooch was concerned as she sized up the little orphan. After three weeks on the road, camping outdoors at night and riding on a horse or in a wagon by day, John looked neglected despite the tender care given him.

"John, the first thing you need is a bath and clean clothes and then a good meal, which is cooking right now. Come with me, Johnnie." Mother Gooch led him into the house for a scrubbing in a copper tub filled with warm water, and then dressed him in brand-new clothes that were just a

little big. "I had to guess at your size for this out-
fit," she explained. She studied him again.

"You and I'll be going to the tailor tomorrow to
measure you for clothes that fit."

When John was soaped, scrubbed and dressed,
Mrs. Gooch led him to the large kitchen table. She
patted the chair next to her at the table as the
family gathered for supper. "Oh, dear," she said,
"He's too short to reach his food."

Colonel Gooch said, "I'll fix that, Matilda." He
left the table and returned with a thick cushion
and plopped John on top of it. John smiled. He
couldn't remember seeing such a wonderful meal.
Hot vegetable soup, potatoes, chicken, beans and
homemade biscuits and apple pie.

He began to feel drowsy, but the three daughters pestered him with questions about the trip
and what he liked to do. "I like to make things and
read, but I'm not very good yet."

"I'll teach you," said Virginia, "tomorrow."

"Tomorrow," John repeated happily. His head
nodded and he struggled to keep his eyes open.

"You look tired, Johnnie," said Mrs. Gooch.
"There will be a lot to do tomorrow. The colonel
wants to show you around the farm . . ."

"And learn to read, please," interrupted John.

Mrs. Gooch gathered him into her arms and carried him to his room. She was so warm and comfort-
ing that by the time she tucked him into bed, he
knew that she was a perfect new mother and that
if he were ever afraid, he could hide behind her

apron for protection. He studied her kind face while she stroked his forehead.

"I know you miss your dear mother, Lucy," said Mrs. Gooch, "but I will try to take good care of you, like she would want me to. We promised your parents that we would."

John felt even more comfortable with his adoptive family after Colonel Gooch took him around the farm the next day to see the cattle and the fields that had been harvested of corn and wheat. The land reminded him of home. On the ride, Colonel Gooch told John that his father had been sad that he had been unable to educate John, to give the boy even a single lesson as he had done with Gideon and Charles.

"As your guardian, I'll make sure that you have the best education. Virginia's your teacher here. She's enrolled in a famous school called the Young Ladies Seminary. She loves books, and learning comes easily for her," the colonel said.

When they returned from the ride, Virginia was waiting in the parlor with her books and a slate for writing. "Tell me what you already know and then we'll start," she said with a smile.

"I know letters," said John. He showed her how he could spell out his name.

"Even if you aren't yet five, I know you'll be the quickest learner ever," she said. "Show me which book we should read first."

It didn't take long for John to feel totally at home with this welcoming family. To his delight, he soon became known around town as Johnnie Gooch. He had become the son that Colonel and Mrs. Gooch had never had, and he was thoroughly happy to be living with them.

Although the child had learned much from Mrs. Gooch and Virginia, including how to recite portions of the Bible and the Sermon on the Mount, Colonel Gooch decided that when John turned eight, it was time for him to go to the white public school.

"I don't think that's a good idea," fretted Mrs. Gooch. "John's so small and it's so far—more than a mile to walk."

"Besides, he's just eight," said Virginia. "He's still learning a lot from me—reading, geography, arithmetic, spelling. I think he should wait till he's older and bigger."

The colonel knew when the battle was not going well with his wife and daughter. He agreed to wait three months before insisting that John enroll.

On a beautiful Monday morning in early 1837, Mrs. Gooch and Virginia watched as John and the colonel, and a hound named Buckeye, left for the mile-long walk to school rooms located in the gallery of the Methodist church. John was excited about the adventure, but also nervous about what to expect. Mrs. Gooch had packed nice things for his lunch—a yam, homemade bread and jam, and a large slice of cake—in his clean and bright new dinner bucket. In his other hand he carried his books. He was proudly wearing his roundabout, a jacket that came to his waist, and Kentucky blue jeans. When Mrs. Gooch had come home with his new school clothes, she had also brought him a fashionable cap and shoes.

Colonel Gooch spoke with the stern and learned principal. The school had two departments, one for the small, less-educated pupils, and the other for older and more advanced ones.

Despite his size and age, he qualified for the advanced group because of Virginia's tutoring.

His teacher was a kindhearted and affectionate woman named Miss Annie Colburn, but her classroom was not what John expected. There were no desks, and the seats were simple slabs of wood on legs—benches with no backs. For six hours a day, with a break for lunch, he and his classmates had to sit on these benches. It was a new and trying experience for John, who had become used to comfort.

John was eager to start school, but later in life he realized that negative school experiences "often handicap and ruin even promising boys and girls."

To make matters worse, when John perched on the bench, his feet didn't touch the floor. His back ached with pain no matter how he twisted or turned. He couldn't get comfortable. After a few days, he needed a plan, and even though he wasn't used to deception, he had to think of something to get away from this discomfort. He waited until he had finished his lunch one day, then said, "Miss Colburn, I can't stay."

"Why not, Johnnie?" she asked, looking up from her book.

"I have to go home at two to help take care of the cows every day," he said, hoping that she would believe him.

"Oh, dear, you'll miss the afternoon classes, but if you must go, then you must. The colonel wouldn't have you go home unless it was important," she said.

John was pleased that she believed him, and headed home after the lunch intermission for an entire week.

But one afternoon Colonel Gooch saw him walking down the towpath along the canal during the time he should have been in class.

"Why are you home so early?" he asked.

John replied quickly, "The teacher lets me come." And for two more days, he got away with his story. Colonel Gooch said that he was going with him the next morning to find out what was going on.

When Miss Colburn told the colonel about Johnnie being needed to help with the cows, the colonel said, "He's not needed at home. His whole business is to attend school. Rules are rules."

Johnnie feared the worst after the colonel left, but sweet Miss Colburn took pity. She asked kindly, "Don't you feel sorry that you told such stories?"

John thought about how uncomfortable the benches were and replied honestly, "No, madam."

Miss Colburn made adjustments to the bench so that he was more comfortable, and John became earnest in his schoolwork.

Unfortunately, his life with the Gooch family was not to last. He learned that the Gooches, like many Ohio farmers at the time, were planning to move to the new state of Missouri where they could buy fertile land more cheaply and increase their wealth. He listened to many conversations at the dinner table as friends and family members debated whether or not they should sell their properties and go west. Mrs. Gooch was initially against the move, but eventually she agreed with the colonel and their sons-in-law. He sold the beautiful farm that John had grown to love, and his other properties, and they prepared to depart. The only way to get to the new state was by canal boat to Portsmouth, then by steamboat to St. Louis.

Everyone in the family had been consulted about the move, except John, until they were almost ready to leave. Then Colonel and Mrs. Gooch, after explaining everything to John asked, "Will you go with us or do you prefer to remain here?"

John, who had come to know these people as his mother and father, promptly answered, "I will go with you."

The Colonel and Mrs. Gooch were overjoyed.

All John's clothing, his dogs, hunting and fishing tackle, his books—everything was packed for the trip. Three days before their departure, they began loading the rented canal boat moored near their house. When their household and personal possessions, two teams of valuable horses and expensive hounds were finally on board, John, Colonel and Mrs. Gooch, their daughters and their husbands, were ready to begin their journey.

John and the Gooches sat on the deck and took one long last look at the farm, with its fields, orchards and garden. He was filled with excitement, but also sadness about leaving home.

When everyone awoke the next day, they were surprised to discover that the boat had only traveled fifteen miles before it went aground because of a break downstream. To pass the time while they waited for repairs, John went ashore and amused himself by throwing pebbles into the water.

Typical Ohio Canal boat, pulled on a towpath by horses or mules, circa 1902. National Register of Historic Places. (public domain)

Linda Salisbury

Suddenly in the distance he saw riders on galloping horses coming toward them down the towpath. He hurried aboard to tell the captain. The riders stopped at the boat and asked to speak with Colonel Gooch. One, a white man was the Ross County sheriff, the other was his half-brother, William.

"Where's John?" demanded William.

Afraid, John slipped behind Mrs. Gooch.

"Why? What do you want?" asked the colonel as he stepped off the boat.

"We have papers," said the sheriff. "John can't leave with you."

"What do you mean?" asked the colonel. "I'm John's guardian. His father appointed me."

"The court will decide if John can go to Missouri with you or if he must stay here in Ohio. You and John must come back to Chillicothe immediately."

"But Johnnie has chosen to go with us," said the colonel with dismay.

"Get the boy!" ordered the sheriff.

When he saw it was no use arguing, the colonel boarded the boat and found his wife. He informed her what was happening and tried to tell her not to worry. John, clinging to her, was filled with dread and alarm as the colonel gently pulled him away. Both John and Mother Gooch sobbed, heartbroken, while the daughters wept. There was no delay, however, and John rode behind the colonel on his horse, holding tightly to the man who had been his father for six years.

At three o'clock, the case was called in the courtroom and the colonel realized he was being charged with trying to kidnap the child. A crowd of blacks and whites gathered, many not understanding why John was going with the Gooches or that the boy's father had appointed the colonel as his guardian. It was rumored that the colonel was kidnapping John so that he could take his inheritance. The shouts of "kidnapper" terrified John. He sat in the courtroom, weeping as if his heart was breaking, as the attorneys on both sides elegantly argued the case.

The judge ruled that John could not leave with the Gooches, and that the colonel had to say good-bye. The overcome colonel showered John with hugs and kisses while John clung to him and sobbed. William restrained John as the colonel finally left.

"Return of John," an illustration from John's autobiography, page 50a.

Linda Salisbury

Later, William tried to explain that he had stopped John from going because he feared that he wouldn't receive as good of an education in Missouri, and was even more concerned that if something happened to Colonel and Mrs. Gooch, John's freedom, as a person of color, would be endangered in a slave-holding state.

John would understand later, but at the time, all he knew was that his beloved Gooches were gone. He wasn't yet ten years old and orphaned a second time.

Raised by a white family and educated in a school for white children in Chillicothe, little Johnnie Gooch had not realized how his mixed-race background could and would affect his future. By law he was considered black.

3

Ruffany in the Streets

JOHN FELT LOST, CONFUSED and alone after the court hearing and the immediate departure of Colonel Gooch. He had lost his father and mother again and was without his best friends. Even before the court hearing William had decided to board John with Richard Long, who had purchased the Gooches' beautiful farm and home and Long would be the boy's new guardian.

John thought living at the farm might make him feel closer to the Gooches, but he had no idea what he was getting into. Perhaps his brothers didn't know either. They explained to John that Mr. Long was an abolitionist, a new word. John asked what it meant and was told that "Mr. Long loves colored people and would have them all treated kindly"—or at least fairly, regardless of color, even though he was a stern man.

As John quickly learned, life in the stone house would be entirely different from when the

Gooches were there. There was no warm greeting for the orphan. No fishing rods or pet dogs. No Mother Gooch to hug him like a son, and no school lessons. Mr. Long was not fatherly like Colonel Gooch had been. He didn't welcome him with a hug and promises to take rides around the fields together. He was from New England and thought that what was most important in life was learning to work hard. He was disappointed that one of his own sons was much like his mother, kindhearted and talented but unwilling to milk a cow, chop the wood or do farm work. So, when John arrived, he saw an opportunity to have him become a farmworker. School was no longer a priority. Life became solemn and earnest.

John was frightened. Even before he found out where to unpack his trunk and where he might sleep, Mr. Long sized him up and said, "What, sir, can you do?"

John replied honestly, "I can't do anything." He had been living a life of leisure with the Gooch family, going to school and fishing. At ten, he hadn't learned a trade—a way to support himself.

Astonished, Mr. Long asked, "How do you expect to live?"

John had no answer. Mr. Long did not look pleased. He said that John would have plenty of work to do on the farm. He wasn't unkind, but that didn't matter.

Fortunately, John loved the horses and became a skilled driver by the time he was eleven. Besides working in the fields, he attended the Presbyterian church with the Longs, driving the team of sorrel horses pulling the carriage filled with family to the Sunday services. In addition to his chores, he studied the Bible and attended Sabbath lessons along with other members of the family.

John often wondered if Mrs. Gooch remembered him and if he'd ever see her again.

It was a new life now, but one that taught him the value of work. He labored hard in the fields, tended the horses, and kept to himself. The physical activity made him strong, perhaps for the first time in his life. He realized later that by staying with this serious family, he was preparing for what he might face later. He would become self-sufficient.

After about a year and a half, there was yet another change. Gideon wanted him to move with him to Cincinnati, Ohio, to attend better schools. John quickly agreed. He was not sorry to leave the Longs.

At that time in Ohio, there were no public schools for black students, only private ones, and not many at that. John was soon enrolled in a private school located in the basement of the Baker Street Baptist Church. His teachers were two white men, Mr. Goodwin and Mr. Denham.

Because Gideon was unmarried, John was boarded with the John Woodson family for the first six months that he lived in the city. Woodson was a black man of "great prominence and influence."

By trade he was a carpenter and a joiner, like John's half-brother, William. He was well educated and superintendent of the Methodist church.

Now that John could study once again his schoolwork improved so much that soon he was in advanced classes and he also became popular among the students. He studied arithmetic and grammar, was involved with plays, and learned to give speeches at various events.

After a few months, he moved from the Woodsons to live with the William Watson family. William Watson was the leading black barber in the city, and John enjoyed his beautiful home and its friendly atmosphere.

The black community in Cincinnati was generally wealthy, well educated and accomplished. John remembers that they "gave striking evidences in every way at this time, of its intelligence, industry, thrift, and progress; and in matters of education and moral and religious culture, furnished an example worthy of the imitation of their whole people."

White troublemakers were prejudiced against the blacks, and were also angry with white abolitionists. A big part of the tension was the city's proximity to Kentucky, a slave state. Fugitive slaves frequently crossed the Ohio River and were hidden or helped by white and black abolitionists. That made the pro-slavery interests seek revenge, leading to violent mobs terrorizing and killing blacks. Although Ohio did not allow slavery, a number of whites were opposed to allowing more blacks to move into the state and, for years, required a $500 bond (which hadn't been enforced) to be posted by black "immigrants" to guarantee "good behavior." That was intimidating to those fleeing to freedom and usually without money.

John witnessed a mob scene that made a lasting impression. "The infuriated rabble" hurled the newspaper printing press belonging to white abolitionist, Dr. Gamaliel Bailey, into the river. Bailey was the editor and publisher of the *Philanthropist*, an antislavery publication. Other abolitionists and friends of the black community were also threatened and feared attacks.

On a Friday in late fall of 1840, a terrible fight broke out when a "ruffany group" from Kentucky, along with their friends from Cincinnati, began

Newspaperman Dr. Gamaliel Bailey, who later founded the antislavery Liberty Party.

As an outspoken abolitionist he was often threatened by people who were in favor of slavery. Three different times unruly mobs broke into his newspaper office and destroyed the printing press. (public domain)

their "outrageous, barbarous and deadly attack" on the entire black community. Blacks were assaulted wherever the mob could find them. During the course of the all-night fight, many whites and blacks were killed or injured.

By Saturday morning, numerous citizens hoped the riot was over, but instead things became worse. Whites were named as police officers with the power to arrest every black man who could be found, just because they had defended themselves. Hundreds of blacks went into hiding to escape arrest and that included William Woodson, with whom John had been living. Woodson hid in the chimney of his house. John's plan was to find Gideon, a barber, who was hiding with the five men who worked for him. Despite his almost-white skin, Gideon was at risk because he was well known for his antislavery activities.

"Be careful, John. Run quietly and hide if necessary. God bless," said Mr. Woodson as he wiggled into the chimney, lifting up his feet so they wouldn't be seen by the attackers.

John's heart was pounding. He left the house through the backyard and garden, jumped the fence into the alley and made his way quickly by Main Street to the canal bridge. He stopped briefly to catch his breath and listen. Then he ran again to the middle of the bridge when suddenly he heard officers shouting, "Stop! Stop!" John was terrified. John remembered Woodson's words that he should run, so he dashed with all his might for more than a mile until he reached Main and Fourth streets, and entered a drugstore that he had to pass through before he could reach his brother's barbershop.

Overcome by exhaustion and the excitement of running for his life, he passed out, as if dead. People in the shop quickly carried him to his brother, where he was revived. John tried to speak, but Gideon put his hand over his mouth. His eyes said, "Silence."

His brother, Gideon, and the others, who were in hiding, had fortified the shop so that ruffians, including the deputized officers, couldn't get in. They were frightened and feared that because John had been pursued, he would be found and they would be arrested.

However, although they didn't know it then, good men, owners of the drugstore, were protecting them against harm. When it was safe to leave the building, the store's employees helped John purchase food for his brother and the other men; none had eaten for more than fifteen hours while hiding.

The continuing ugliness and violence did not stop the antislavery sentiment or activities in this city or the state of Ohio. Abolitionists became bolder and stronger, and so did the black citizens. John remembers that, "Nor did such treatment close the lips and hush the voices of the eloquent colored men themselves, who through such experiences were learning what their rights were, and how to advocate and defend them." He was impressed by powerful orators, including Gideon, who spoke about freedom and rights.

On the Sunday after the "dark days" of the riots, the city was quiet, but the so-called police were still everywhere and John was terrified of the "awful tread and tramp of their march."

He no longer felt safe in Cincinnati's streets after this time of violence.

~ ~ ~

After John had attended school for about a year in Cincinnati, Colonel Gooch made a surprise visit. He was returning from Chillicothe where he had been finalizing the sale of his properties, and had hoped to find John there. When he learned that John was gone, he tracked him down in his new location. After all, the colonel's wife and Virginia had insisted that he report back to them about how John was doing.

John heard a knock on the school door and a familiar voice ask, "Have you a young boy in your school by the name of John Mercer Langston?"

To John's delight, it was the colonel, who threw his fatherly arms around him. He took John's hand, and placed his other arm around the boy's neck and shoulder and they walked together to the school yard where they sat. Colonel Gooch drew John close to him so that the boy's head was on his shoulder.

"It was awful leaving without you," he said. "Everyone wept."

John wanted to tell him how he felt abandoned and betrayed, but he was afraid of saying too much.

They talked for two hours, first about Mrs. Gooch and his "sister" Virginia. "They miss you terribly and speak of you all the time," said the colonel. "They wonder how you are doing and if you are happy."

What could he say? John didn't want them to worry.

"Is your house as nice as the stone house?" John asked, to change the subject.

"It and the land are beautiful," the colonel replied. "The new farm is larger and valuable because the area is being settled rapidly with good people." Then he said he wanted John to promise one thing that would make Mrs. Gooch and Virginia happy.

"Yes, anything," said John, his eyes shining.

"Promise that when you are of age you will come to us and make yourself at home with your best friends. You must come!"

John promised. They had been wonderful and devoted parents to him. He especially loved Mrs. Gooch. Yes, he would find her when he was old enough.

However, by the time he was of age at twenty-one, John had learned more about Missouri and knew that he didn't want to travel there even briefly. It was still a slave state and his personal liberty could be in danger because he was considered black. It would be dangerous to even visit.

51

He waited to try to find the Gooch family until after slavery was abolished, but sadly no one in Gooch family could be located anywhere.

During the two years that John was in Cincinnati, and lived with William Watson, he attended school five days a week, and on Saturdays he worked in the barbershop and at a bathhouse, where he received tips. The tips were often large because he was helpful and polite. His adult friends taught him about business and encouraged him to save his money. On Sundays he went to church with the Watsons.

His life would change again when he returned to Chillicothe for the settling of his father's estate. Because he was still a boy, he had to name a guardian for himself and his property. Gideon was still in Cincinnati, and Charles was a student at Oberlin College in Northern Ohio.

John named his half-brother, William, whom he loved greatly, to be in charge of himself and his portion of the estate. He was fond of William, who had often visited him wherever he lived and often brought him presents.

This would mean living in Chillicothe once again. Because William wasn't married, as was the custom of the time, he boarded John with friends from Virginia who could attend to his daily needs, such as fixing meals and getting him off to school. The friends said that the Commonwealth of Virginia "supplied the best looking, the best behaved, the most excellent men and women, boys and girls."

Soon John began school again. His teachers, George B. Vashon, and later, William Cuthbert, were black students at Oberlin College. John and the other students were impressed by both men.

The more John learned from them, the more he knew that he wanted to further his education at their college. Charles enthusiastically agreed. He had just returned to Chillicothe and told everyone that John was "smart and promising and should be as thoroughly educated as might be."

Gideon wrote a letter of agreement. He knew that Oberlin offered excellent opportunities as Oberlin, founded in 1833, was the first college in the nation to admit black students (1835), then the first college to admit women (1837). Charles and Gideon were its first black students.

His half-brother, William, wasn't convinced, but he finally agreed to let John go for one year to Oberlin's preparatory school where he would take college courses. But he also felt that John had already had an adequate education. "What he needs is a trade," he said.

John had excelled once again and even won William's praise when at the end of the term, he gave his declamation—forcefully expressing his opinions.

"Well done, Brother," said William, beaming. "Well done. Your father would be proud."

Charles went even further. "You have in you, John, all the elements of a great orator."

John was fourteen.

4

Learning and Labor

John was delighted to be heading off to Oberlin with his teacher, George Vashon. It would give him a chance to talk more about what to expect at the school preparing him for college, and the town's reputation in the antislavery movement, particularly for helping fugitive slaves. They left Chillicothe on Thursday, March 1, 1844, traveling about 150 miles on difficult roads.

George described the gristmills and sawmills along Plum Creek, and told him that the college trustees planted 39,000 mulberry trees to attract silkworms that would spin fibers to make silk. Silk would provide new jobs, they had hoped.

"The plan failed," said George. "Most of the trees were eaten by cattle or killed by drought. Oberlin's a beautiful place, though, and filled with people with ideas and values. And you'll find many folks who'll risk their lives to help others."

"So I've heard from Charles," said John. "I know Oberlin's a station on the underground railroad. I plan to help with the fugitives. It's a promise I made to an old friend."

The last forty-eight miles from Mansfield to the college town were especially rough and almost impassible because of deep mud. They finally hired a horse and wagon, which John knew was an extravagance.

They arrived in Oberlin on Sunday morning and found the roads and plank walkways were wet and muddy. Soon they saw townspeople, looking neither left nor right, as they headed silently for early prayer meetings. By 10:30, the crowd had grown even larger as students, faculty, and villagers walked solemnly to the new brick First Church.

George said, "John, wait until you hear the preacher. What a sermon he'll give! It's always thrilling."

After they slipped into seats, John was enthralled by the singing and the sound of the great choir of more than 100 voices. It moved his soul. And then came the scripture lesson led by Professor John Morgan. John forgot about the long and difficult journey and his mud-caked shoes as his mind was lifted to new ideas. He was particularly

First Congregational Church in Oberlin, Ohio, on National Register of Historic Places.

Linda Salisbury

The Reverend Charles Grandison Finney was an evangelist and second president of Oberlin College (1851–1856). He was also a professor at Oberlin Theological Seminary and was pastor of First Congregational Church, built from 1843–44. When asked by Arthur Tappan, who provided financial backing to start Oberlin College, Finney accepted as long as he could continue preaching in New York State, and he wanted assurance that Oberlin would guarantee free speech. (photo, public domain)

pleased that the lesson was based on the Sermon on the Mount, initially taught to him by Virginia Gooch. Oh, if she could hear this lesson! When the professor read the passage about considering the lilies, John realized that he was not the only person moved. Tears flowed down many cheeks. Then came the oration by the Reverend Charles G. Finney, one of the college founders. He spoke for an hour and a half, as the congregation listened intently. It wasn't surprising that everyone, including the children, returned to hear Reverend Finney preach again in the afternoon. After his talk, everyone left in silence, so deeply moved were they by the preacher's words.

John cleared his throat and said, "George, I've never heard anything like this. His oration was like mighty storms that I imagine on the sea and in the mountains."

George smiled and clapped John on the shoulder. "Welcome to Oberlin."

The following day, rested from their travels, John paid the school for his tuition and expenses. He was asked what he planned to study, English, or Greek and Latin. When John hesitated, George quickly answered, "He will study Greek and Latin taking up the grammar of those languages at once."

That settled things and John began his studies, but only after he met Professor and Mrs. George Whipple. Professor Whipple taught mathematics and he and his wife were willing to let John board with them. They also agreed to serve as his guardian while in school. John was impressed by both the Whipples and their daughter, who was in many of his classes.

After George brought John's trunk to the door, he was shown to his room. He had barely looked around and unpacked when it was time for dinner. The chairs were filled with members of the Whipple family and other boarders. There was only one seat left at the table. John, the newcomer, found himself near Mrs. Whipple and a teacher and scholar, Mary True. The women asked him so many questions that he barely had a chance to eat.

It didn't take long for John to feel fully at home, and his time in Oberlin's preparatory program passed much too quickly. He had studied hard in Greek and Latin, advanced arithmetic, and algebra, Bible lessons and rhetoric, and was ready to enter the college itself. After the fall term was over, he told his professors and friends good-bye, and said that he expected to return to Oberlin in the spring of 1845.

But it was not to happen as planned. While he was staying for two weeks in Chillicothe with Charles, a committee of black men arrived from the Hicks Settlement about eight miles away to ask Charles to help them find a schoolteacher for their children during the winter months—from November to February. They would pay the teacher ten dollars per month in cash and provide board by having the teacher stay a week with each student's family.

After thinking for a moment, Charles said, "I really don't know anyone."

"What about your brother?" asked one man.

Charles replied, "Frankly, he's young, and even though John is accomplished, I'm not sure he's ready to teach and manage your school."

The men talked among themselves, then one said, "Charles, the students are mostly young men and young girls. They work hard in their studies and are well behaved. The work of the teacher is mostly listening to their recitations and teaching basic spelling, reading, arithmetic, geography and writing."

Charles called John in to hear the committee's proposal, and he agreed to become the teacher. He was still fifteen.

When John walked into the classroom, he realized that he was the smallest person in the room, except for a boy named Samuel Cox. Despite his size, John had no problems with discipline. All his students were eager to learn. In addition to teaching in the school, John was asked by a prominent local resident, John Jackson, to educate his son, who was too young to attend the school. For this extra work, five miles from the settlement, Jackson boarded John with his family and took care of his horse. And Jackson became a second student in that house because he wanted to have an education as well.

John was paid monthly by the families because there were still no pubic schools for black students. The ten dollars often consisted of five- and ten-cent pieces, plus coppers, and occasionally a twenty-five cent piece. Because his meals and housing were provided by the families, John had no other expenses and was able to save his $35 earnings.

After the school term was over he went back to the Jacksons' house to say good-bye, counted his money and wrapped it in a white pocket handkerchief. As he went downstairs, he was surprised to see members of the school committee waiting to thank him once again.

Then it was time to leave. He handed his small sack of money to John Jackson to hold while he mounted his horse. Mr. Jackson smiled. John knew that small white handkerchief's contents were bulky because of the coins even if the total was not that great. But it was his, and he had earned all of it himself. John was becoming even more self-reliant.

He hadn't been back in Chillicothe very long when he was asked to teach at yet another school.

Oberlin's students had a long winter vacation during which many students taught or did other work that helped them pay for their education and to be useful in society.

Samuel Deveaux, who had become the teacher of the city's black school after George Vashon had returned to Oberlin, was looking for someone to take his place for a short time.

"Charles," he asked, "will you teach these students?"

Charles quickly replied, "I can't do it, but John is the teacher of our family. He has just accomplished what he considers a feat in teaching the school in Hicks Settlement, and his success there has made him quite bold enough and self-reliant to attempt almost anything in the line of school teaching."

John listened quietly, but wasn't happy about the way Charles had described him. It sounded like his brother was making fun of him. Before he could say anything in his defense, Deveaux turned to him and said he'd pay him as a substitute for two weeks of work. John was uncomfortable about taking on a job that would mean teaching students who had been his playmates when he was growing up at the Gooch farm. He knew that some of these students were troublemakers and might be hard to manage, even though he could teach them the material.

Deveaux wouldn't take no for an answer, so John finally agreed to teach for two weeks, three weeks at the most, until the teacher returned.

For the most part, the teaching went well. Students, particularly in the advanced classes, welcomed him and he didn't have discipline problems except for one. He had to punish one of the smartest and smallest boys, who was mischievous.

When the time was up, John proudly added twenty dollars to his savings, and he decided that he wanted to do even greater things.

But he faced a major obstacle. His lovable half-brother William was still his guardian. William had given John permission to attend the Oberlin prep school for a year, but that was all. William, who had not received the same kind of academic training, thought that John needed to take up a trade as he had done. Once William had made up his mind, he could be stubborn.

Even though young John was aware of William's views on learning a trade, such as carpentry, he really hadn't expected him to be quite so opposed to his returning to college. After all, John had done well as a student at Oberlin and as a teacher. He had proven his abilities as a scholar and by his love of education.

John was worried and depressed that he wouldn't be allowed to return to college, but Charles was the first person to come to his aid and to keep him from a life of ordinary mechanical labor.

Charles knew that their father, Ralph Quarles, wanted his sons to be safe and well educated. He took up the cause with William. "He should become a carpenter, like me," argued William.

"You know what Father and our mother wanted for us," said Charles. "He set aside money for our education."

William wasn't convinced.

The second person who spoke in favor of John's return to Oberlin was Professor Whipple, who wrote a letter to John through William. The professor said that John should return to college and complete a degree. William finally gave in. He said, "John, you will decide for yourself."

Overjoyed and without hesitation, John said that he wanted to return to Oberlin.

William was still concerned about John's future after college, and asked, "Then what will you do?"

Charles interrupted, "Time will take care of the boy's interests."

It was settled and John prepared to go back to school, this time by stagecoach. The coach ran from Chillicothe through the state capital of Columbus, where John got off to stay the night and have supper at the Neil House, the main hotel.

As John entered the building on a dark and rainy March night in 1845, a rude clerk told him that he couldn't come inside because of his skin color and he would have to find a different lodging.

John couldn't believe what he was hearing. He felt outcast and heartbroken. He didn't know what to do or where to go. A black man passing by asked, "What's the matter?" and after John explained his situation, the man kindly said, "Follow me," and took him to a home where he was well cared for that night.

But his encounter with the rude hotel clerk was not yet over as John discovered the next day. When he returned to the coach, the clerk, who was working for the coach company, told him to sit, not inside with the other passengers, but up in the rain with the driver. John, a paying passenger, responded, "I will do no such thing."

Another passenger who had seen what had happened both the night before and at this moment said to the agent, "No! He will not take a seat upon the outside of the coach."

The man then stepped out of the coach and urged all the other passengers to do the same. He said they would return to their seats as their names were called out by the agent from the clerk's list in the order in which tickets had been purchased. John's was first on the list. He climbed inside and was able to sit next to the man who had defended him. For the rest of the journey, his color did not make a difference in how he was treated.

Although John excelled in his studies, his start in oratory at Oberlin did not begin well when the president of The Union Society asked him to participate in a debate. John prepared for it but when the moment came to speak on the topic, of "Do the teachings of phrenology interfere with man's sense of moral agony?" he froze. He only got as far as saying, "Mr. President . . . " John recalled that "every thought, every feeling, every mental experience and condition, with every word he had ever known took wings and flew away, leaving his mind a complete blank."

How embarrassing! His heart sank when he returned to his chair, and tears fell. Classmates tried to console him when the event was over. Their sympathy only made things worse. John, in his humiliation and feeling like a total failure, hurried away to avoid everyone and went back to his room in Tappan Hall. A flood of tears continued to fall as he locked his door and threw himself on his bed. His pillow and bed were soaked from his tears. With his eyes puffy and red, he finally stood up and looked in his mirror and then made the most solemn vow of his life. "With God's help I will never fail again in any effort at making a speech." He was determined to improve and succeed.

The next morning, he was stopped on the street by a young man, who was a member of the same debating society. The fellow said, "Langston, I have to go home for the week and I want you to take my place in the society debate next Thursday evening. Don't say no. Do it for me."

With new resolve, John replied, "I'll do so."

When he appeared at the debate, he was introduced as the substitute. John did so well that he was given extra time and did well. He had fulfilled his vow and studied earnestly. In August of 1849, Asa Mahan, the college's first president, presented John's diploma. He had proven that he was both an excellent debater and writer, and he was graduated with high honors.

After receiving his college degree, John's dream was to attend law school. He was twenty and, at twenty-one, he would no longer be under the watchful eye and decision-making of William, even though William and John's friends now encouraged him to continue with his education. John knew that there were no black lawyers in Ohio. Public sentiment seemed to be against having blacks in office, as attorneys, or working in other professions. Courts and juries consisted of white men. Blacks knew that they faced prejudice both in the courts and in the ways that laws were written both in Ohio and around the nation.

John realized that becoming a lawyer was not going to be easy. *Where can I study law?* he wondered. *Who will take me as a student and give me instruction and attention that I will need, even though I have a college degree and I'm a citizen of the United States, and the state of Ohio?*

An older black man advised John that it would be absurd to study law. "It's something that only the smartest white men can do with success," he warned.

About the same time, a white antislavery attorney answered a letter that John had sent him about working in his law office. The man said he couldn't take John in his office and encouraged him to move to the British West Indies. He said that John could learn law and practice there.

That was not what John wanted to do, and he tried to find a place to study law in the United States. He applied to Ballston Spa law school in New York State, where a friend was a student.

John wrote to John Fowler, who owned and ran the school. In his letter John was honest about his qualifications, his character, his race, and complexion, and he explained that he could afford to pay for his education and would provide good references. Fowler discussed his request with the trustees and the faculty and they responded that they wouldn't admit John because of his color. However, Fowler suggested that if John came in person to the school, perhaps those opposing him would change their minds if they saw him.

John traveled more than 500 miles to give Fowler his application. Fowler said he would submit it to the faculty and trustees. Twenty-four hours later, Fowler met John at his hotel and explained that he once again had been denied admission because of his color. Fowler further explained that a Mr. John C. Calhoun, of South Carolina, had been on campus during graduation a year earlier and had promised to encourage more students from his state to enroll, but only if blacks were denied admission so these white students would not be offended.

John was stunned and saddened, and said, "I'm sorry to hear that."

Fowler could see how upset John was and said, "You have my sympathy. I would be pleased to do something to help you in your studies."

Then Fowler paused and added, "I'll tell you what I'll do. I'll let you *edge* your way into my school." He thought another moment and added,

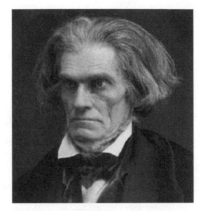

John C. Calhoun, of South Carolina, a senator, vice president, and supporter of slavery. (Mathew Brady photo, public domain.)

"John, if you'll consent to pass as a Frenchman or a Spaniard hailing from the West India Islands in Central or South America, I will take you into the school."

John was astonished. He couldn't believe what he had just heard. "What do you mean by 'edge your way' into the school?"

Fowler said, "Well, you'd come into the classrooms, take your seat and sit apart from the class, ask no questions, behave yourself quietly, and if, after a time, no one says anything against you, you can move up nearer the class and then in time become a full member of the class."

Fowler seemed to hope that this would be a solution because he knew John was more than well-qualified to study in his school. He apparently had no idea how humiliating this suggestion would be to John Mercer Langston.

John rose from his seat and faced the man he knew was trying to help him, even though the proposal was totally unacceptable.

He said respectfully, "Mr. Fowler, I thank you. But, however much I may desire to enter your school, I will do so upon no terms or conditions of humiliation. I will not *edge* my way into your institution. Nor will I yield my American birthright, as a Frenchman or Spaniard, to gain that object!"

"I was born in Virginia and upon a plantation. Neither of these facts will I deny. I expect to live as I hope to die in my own country in the service of my own fellow citizens! Mr. Fowler, before I would consent to the humiliation and degradation implied in either of your propositions, I would open my veins and die of my own act. I am a colored American, and I shall not prove false to myself, nor neglect the obligation I owe to the Negro race. You will pardon the vehemence and positiveness of my utterance."

John stood taller than ever before, and his words reflected his firm beliefs and his ability as an orator. Fowler's face was kind as he had listened intently, but he shook his head and said, "Mr. Langston, you have my sympathy, but I cannot take you as a student."

To that John promptly replied, "I do not need sympathy, Mr. Fowler. I need the privilege of your law school."

Fowler was about to say farewell, when he had another thought. "Mr. Langston, don't you give lectures sometimes? Would you like to give one here in our large lecture room?"

"I would," said John.

"What would you talk about?" asked Fowler.

"Your treatment of a young, educated colored man, the first of his class to ask admission as a student to any American law school," John said firmly.

Fowler was taken aback, quickly withdrew his offer for John to speak at the school, and hurriedly said good-bye.

John returned to Ohio, applied for admission at a law school in Cincinnati, and was also denied, again because of his race.

Judge Timothy Walter, who conducted that school, said he couldn't admit John "because his students would not feel at home with him, and he would not feel at home with them."

It was time to take a new approach to becoming an attorney.

5

Two Degrees, and First Election

DESPITE THE REBUFFS from two law schools, John was not about to give up on his dream of becoming a lawyer. If anything, he was even more determined. He decided to seek advice from Oberlin Professor John Morgan, whom he liked and trusted. John and many other Oberlin students knew him as a kindhearted scholar, taking a fatherly interest in helping students.

Morgan suggested that John prepare for the law by getting a degree in theology, the study of religion.

Oberlin professor and mentor, John Morgan, who gave John excellent advice. (Permission, Oberlin College Archives.)

"You will develop many skills that will serve you well in the courtroom," said the professor.

So, John applied to Oberlin's Theological Seminary where he would take a three-year course and earn a master's degree in theology.

John Mercer Langston daguerreotype upon graduating from the Oberlin Theological Seminary in 1853. (Permission, Oberlin College Archives.)

He was glad to be back in the college town, and studied with great enthusiasm under distinguished professors, such as Charles G. Finney, John Morgan, Henry Cowles, Henry Peck, and their assistants.

Most important, perhaps, was developing his talents as a public speaker, through courses in rhetoric and by giving sermons. His ability to use words to explain and convince would help him someday in the courtroom when he had to argue before judges and juries. He was eager to become skilled in using logic and solving problems.

He also had the distinction of being the first black seminary student in the nation. At the time, there were still some people who wondered if blacks were as capable of learning as whites, and they asked John's professors what they thought about him. His teachers and fellow students knew these questions were absurd. John not only did well, he was singled out by Professor Finney at graduation as someone to whom he would like to give two degrees if he could. "You deserve them," Professor Finney said, to the applause of John's fellow students. Of course, the professor had hoped and had urged John to become a preacher,

Because of John's reputation and promise, Judge Philomen Bliss prepared John to become the first black man to pass the Ohio Bar. John was only the third black attorney in the United States. (public domain)

but John had other plans. He applied to become a law clerk and student under Judge Philemon Bliss of Elyria, Ohio, near Oberlin. Not only was he accepted because of his reputation and future promise, he was also invited to board in the judge's home. Mrs. Bliss was delighted to have John stay with the family, and didn't care what anyone in the town thought about it.

John began to study the law, and his speaking abilities were soon put to the test once again. He heard a member of the American Colonization Society speak at one of the churches as part of a fundraising campaign for that organization. The society wanted to send blacks to Africa to live instead of dealing with the issue of slavery. John and his brother, Charles had been active in many antislavery meetings and wanted blacks to have full citizenship, not to be sent away from the States.

John asked permission to give his own talk and urged people not to donate money until they heard him speak. He shouldn't have been worried about how his talk would be received—it was successful, and several newspapers wrote about it. Soon, other groups asked him to speak on the topic.

Although Ohio was a free state, there were many so-called Black Laws that restricted the rights of blacks, even those who were free. The laws involved employment, travel, and voting, plus other unfair restrictions. The more John studied law, the more worried he became about passing the exam and becoming a lawyer, but Judge Bliss assured him that he would help him succeed. The judge advised him to attend both civil and criminal courts regularly. He also encouraged John to ask numerous questions, which John did.

After two years of studying law under Judge Bliss, and credited with one of his years of study in the Theological Seminary, John was ready to take the bar exam.

On September 13, 1854, John met with a committee of three attorneys. Two were not pleased that a black man wanted to practice law in Ohio. After they had individually asked all their questions for the examination, they agreed that John had done well. They reported this to the five judges, who would make the decision, and that John was a person of color.

There was discussion among them about John's race, until finally they asked him to stand. Because of his light skin, the panel

Illustration from John's autobiography titled "Admission to the Ohio Bar, 1854," found on page 124b.

agreed he could be considered white. He was admitted to the Ohio Bar that day. He wasn't sure, however, if he would ever be allowed to put his skills to use in court.

In January 1856, John had entered into a purchase agreement for a beautiful fifty-acre farm on South Claus Road in Brownhelm Township, nine miles from Oberlin. In late March, six months before his bar exam, John made the final payment of $3,000 on the property.

In addition to his own earnings from his boyhood, he had a decent inheritance from his father after the Louisa plantation and its assets were sold. He was self-reliant.

He rented his farm and house to an English family—Tom Slater, his wife and their son, John. Besides the two-story frame house, the farm included a barn, orchards, fields and other buildings.

John, now twenty-four, was exhausted to the point that his friends were worried about his health. On doctor's orders the newly accredited attorney decided in September to move to the farm, and live with his white tenants, and his wife, Caroline Wall, whom he married in October. The agreement was that the Slaters would provide room and board for him and do his washing and mending. The Slaters would farm the land and divide the profits with John.

John lived there two years, working and exercising in the open air to regain his health. The lush, though flat, land reminded him of where he had lived with the Gooches, so many years earlier. The meadows were beautiful and there were plenty of trees to be used for fences and buildings. He grew timothy to feed the cattle and sheep in the winter. The property had orchards with many varieties of fruit, including apples, cherries, quinces, pears, peaches and plums, which were sold for extra money. The farm's beauty and abundance made John feel totally at home.

He had been warned by the previous owner that there was one person in the neighborhood who might cause trouble because their properties shared a common boundary, but the lane between their land was on John's side. Colonel Elisha Franklin Peck, the postmaster, frequently used the lane to ride from his large white house and barns to town. As the story goes, John was working in a potato field when the colonel came riding down the road. Rather than wait for trouble, John decided to greet his neighbor even though he had been told that the colonel hated abolitionists, Oberlin, and blacks. But, the colonel was his neighbor, and John preferred to be neighborly.

"Good morning, Colonel Peck!" called out John.

The man replied gruffly, "Who are you?"

John introduced himself and told him where he was from and where he had gone to school. As he expected, he then had to listen to the fellow rant about his background (especially about Oberlin—that awful abolitionist school), and said he wanted nothing to do with John.

John wasn't easily frightened or discouraged. He leaned against a fence post and listened. When his neighbor finished and was about to huff off, John calmly defended Oberlin, and suggested that the colonel's sons and daughters would benefit from such a fine education.

Although this first meeting didn't go well, and although they never agreed politically, they became good neighbors and friends. John was even able to take William Neil, a visiting black abolitionist, to the Pecks' home and they talked together for hours.

John settled into the country life that he had loved from the time he was a boy on the Virginia plantation, then later in Chillicothe. His long rest had restored his health. But things were about to change when a white stranger stopped by. John and the young Slater boy were harvesting the previous year's turnip crop when the man approached them and asked for Lawyer Langston. John decided to play a little joke. He told the stranger that he would find Lawyer Langston in the house and took him there, leaving him in the parlor while he went to his room, cleaned up and dressed in his Sunday clothes. John then made his appearance. "I am Mr. Langston," he announced with a smile.

The visitor was in fact attorney Hamilton Perry who, without a reaction, said, "John, I would like you to be my assistant in a court case."

John quickly sat down, his heart pounding, and leaned forward.

Perry placed his hat in his lap and said, "John, this case, involving a property dispute, is expected to attract a large crowd. I think this will give you a chance to show everyone your legal abilities while assisting me. We'll be up against an excellent opponent but you are an excellent debater. Can I count on you?"

John truly hadn't expected to be able to practice law because of his race, even though he had passed the bar. He had new hope for his future in the courtroom.

"I'd be honored," John said. "When shall I begin?"

"Come by my office tomorrow, and we'll go over the details of the case," said Perry.

John's mind raced as he watched the horse and rider gallop off. Tomorrow couldn't come soon enough.

Perry was correct. So many people wanted to attend the trial by jury that the court officials had to find a larger area—a barn—to accommodate the crowd. John made the eloquent closing arguments for the defendant, and the jury unanimously agreed with him. No attorney could ever have been happier than John was when he left the courtroom after his first trial. But would there be another chance or was this just a lucky opportunity? Despite all the congratulations, he wasn't sure.

The Slaters prepared a celebratory dinner when they returned at midnight, including serving Mrs. Slater's best "cups of tea."

While he was eating breakfast the next morning, John heard a knock on the front door. A man had come to ask if he would be his attorney.

"I heard how you did in court yesterday," the man said. "I need your help, sir. And I can pay." The man told John about the charges against him. "Please, sir," he pleaded.

"Of course," said John, with a smile.

Then, just few minutes after the first man left, there was another knock, and then another. All day people came to ask John to represent them and each gave him a retainer, a down payment, on his services. Each had either been in the courtroom, waiting outside, or had heard about John's success at the trial. The number of cases continued to grow so rapidly in the days that followed, he gave up the idea of simply farming.

His new clients were white, Irish, English, Americans and they came from several counties nearby. They also paid him well for his services. It didn't take long for him to build his law practice, and his wealth.

His country home was elegant and he had many friends—both white and black—who visited there, sometimes for weeks at a time. He also was frequently asked to speak about social equality and freedom. It was a topic important to him, and when sometimes members of the audience screamed insults at him or about Oberlin College—because of the school's fair treatment of black people—he handled it well and often with humor.

When he arrived at the farm as a single, popular and handsome young man, people wondered
why he hadn't yet married. They didn't realize that
John often left his home in the hands of the Slaters
and went by horse and buggy back to Oberlin to
spend the night with friends. He also visited the
beautiful Caroline "Carrie" Wall, a senior in the
Ladies' Department of the college. John had met
her at Oberlin in 1851, and later at her home in

Caroline Matilda Wall (public domain)

Harveysburg, Ohio, when he had traveled to the town a year later to help black youth obtain better educational opportunities in the state.

Her background was somewhat similar to his: her father was a white wealthy planation-owner, who emancipated her (but not her enslaved mother). He had sent Carrie and her siblings from North Carolina to live with Quakers in Harveysburg, and made sure she had a good education and a generous inheritance.

John was impressed not only by her beauty but also her intelligence and talents. She was strong-willed and stood up for what was right. And like John and Charles, she and her brother, Orindatus Simon Bolivar "O.S.B." Wall, were active in the Ohio antislavery movement.

John was in love, but in accordance with how things were done at the time, he couldn't propose to her directly. Instead, he had to find a surrogate. So a friend delivered John's letter proposing marriage to Carrie, and her answer was yes.

Mercer and "Sister Carrie," as they addressed each other, were married by Professor Morgan in Oberlin on October 25, 1854, and eventually became the devoted parents of five children.

In March 1855, local towns were selecting candidates to run for various offices. As a black man, John was not allowed to vote, but he was deeply interested in politics. He attended and spoke at political meetings with other residents who were fighting to end slavery. He actively campaigned for black suffrage—the right to vote. His friend Charles Fairchild, encouraged him to attend the Liberty Party's meetings in March where the party's candidates would be chosen. Fairchild was one of the original settlers of Brownhelm, and the brother of Oberlin professor and later college president, James H. Fairchild. Then came the surprise. Fairchild said, "I intend to nominate you, John, for Brownhelm clerk. It's a position that entails many legal duties."

John was honored, but he had concerns. He answered, "That would be a risk for the party. We should nominate someone who could be elected."

Fairchild said, "You're the most qualified. And, I believe you *can* be elected."

John was grateful that Fairchild had only mentioned his qualifications and not his race, but he still had concerns. "You know that no colored man has ever been elected as a public official in the entire country."

His friends knew that was true, but when they insisted that he be nominated for the clerk of Brownhelm Township, he finally agreed. In April, when the votes were counted, John was declared the winner by sixty votes. Not surprisingly, his election also helped his law business.

When he returned to the farm after the votes were counted, he and Carrie celebrated with friends. She wrapped her arms around him and whispered, "You're the most qualified, and I'm glad that voters knew it."

John whispered back, "I'm proud to serve."

He had barely settled into his new position when his fame as an orator led to an invitation to speak at American Anti-Slavery Society anniversary meeting in New York City—and they would pay him $50 for just thirty minutes of oratory.

He was honored by the invitation, but most impressed by the other famous speakers who would also be giving orations.

"Did you see the list of names?" he asked his wife. "They're all so well-known."

"You'll do well," she said. "You always do and it's important to be there among them." Her face beamed with pride.

"I will think about you all the time, and worrying. The baby will be here soon. Perhaps I shouldn't go just now," said John, reaching for her hands.

"You must go, Mercer," said Carrie. "Continue to plead the cause of freedom. Friends will look after me."

In May 1855, hundreds filled the Metropolitan Theater to hear famous abolitionists, such as Henry Ward Beecher, Lucretia Mott and Lucy Stone, among others, to denounce the evils of slavery. Introduced by William Lloyd Garrison, society president, John received an ovation for his stirring talk attacking slavery, and those who defended or tolerated the unfairness of unequal education and injustices even in free states.

"American slavery has corrupted the whole mass of American society," John said. He added that because of the Constitution and Declaration of Independence and other documents, "we verily believe that we are a free people; and yet I am forced to declare, looking the truth directly in the face and seeing the power of American slavery, that there is not within the bosom of this entire country, a solitary man or woman who can say 'I have my full share of liberty . . .' "

He addressed, as did other speakers, including Lucy Stone, the horror of slavery in the nation's capital, and noted that Stone had said as a result of slavery, she and others would not go to Washington, D.C., or hold a future antislavery convention there. He condemned the treatment of blacks in Ohio, where in all aspects of society, from public education to imprisonment, blacks were treated as inferiors.

Slavery would die when people willed it. But "as long as the Church and political parties bow down at its bloody feet to worship it, it will live and breathe, active and invincible," he argued.

He thundered on, "Shall liberty die in this country?. . . The question is with us, shall the Declaration of American Independence stand? Shall the Constitution of the United States, if it is antislavery, stand? Shall our free institutions triumph, and our country become the asylum of the oppressed of all climes? . . . May God help the right."

6
Dramatic Rescue

JOHN RETURNED TO HIS FARM, exhausted from the almost 1,000-mile-round trip to New York City. His head was still filled with the sights—the shops, noise, crowds, and dirt, were compared with beautiful, peaceful Brownhelm.

Carrie was waiting at the door when he rode up and Tom Slater led his horse to the barn to be watered, fed and washed down.

"I need to be fed and washed, too, Sister Carrie," said John giving her a hug. "You look wonderful, but tired."

"It won't be long before the baby's here, Mercer," she said. "William's making a cradle for the baby, and my friends have sewn clothes. The doctor said I need to rest and, guess what? Colonel Peck said he will look after me as if I were his own daughter."

"He's turned out to be a great neighbor," said John, still amazed by the change in the man.

On August 3, 1855, their son was born and everyone tried to come up with the perfect name. John asked Charles for suggestions. Since no one could agree on a single name, they decided to give the baby two and finally, after much discussion, the boy was named Arthur, for one of Ralph Quarles' slaves whom John remembered liking for his humor, and Dessalines, for the great Haitian hero and abolitionist. So it was: Arthur Dessalines Langston.

The baby would not grow up in Brownhelm, however. John had decided to trade the farm to O.S.B. Wall, in exchange for a house and lot in the village of Oberlin where there were more opportunities, and his law practice could continue grow.

They left the farm on a beautiful sunny day in the spring of 1856. The team of sorrel horses pulled the wagon along the roads, which were in terrible condition, to 207 E. College Street in the nicest section of town. Most neighbors quickly welcomed them and offered to help Carrie with the baby.

This large, modern house, where the Langstons lived for the next fifteen years, had a cellar, kitchen, dining, and sitting rooms, halls, and parlor, and there were upstairs bedrooms. Large windows added sunlight, and a veranda provided outside seating.

"It's perfect," said Carrie. "There's so much room for us and Arthur, and later more children."

John smiled and said, "But, Sister Carrie, first we need to unpack."

Oberlin and Brownhelm Township were close enough that their friends, including Colonel Peck and his family, often visited, and people from the township continued to ask John to be their attorney.

Shortly after they were settled in their new home, villagers saw the new sign in front of John's law office on North Main Street: JOHN M. LANGSTON, ATTORNEY AND COUNSELLOR AT LAW, SOLICITOR IN CHANCERY AND NOTARY PUBLIC."

Undated photo of Langston home, a National Historic Landmark, on East College Street in Oberlin. (Permission, Oberlin College Archives.)

For seven years after his admission to the bar, John had no clients of color. Part of the problem, John realized, was because under Ohio law, all courts and juries were white, and many serving in them were prejudiced against blacks. No black or mixed-race person was allowed to testify against any white person, if the that person objected. Black people weren't sure what would happen to them in a courtroom if their attorney was also of color.

One day a black man came to his office and in-sisted that John represent him in court. John ac-cepted the case. On the other side was a firm with well-known white lawyers from another county. John's client was accused of stealing cattle. Threats were made. His client was told that nei-ther he nor his "colored attorney" should dare to show up in court. Both John and his client refused to be intimidated and they arrived at the court-house. They heard insults both outside and inside the courtroom, but John's oration turned the crowd around so that he gained sympathy and applause from bystanders. And he won the case.

The insults continued at other trials, and in one situation, John finally had had it with the other side's client, who was wandering around the court-house and saying nasty things. John struck him with his fist and the man fell to the floor. Every-one waited to see what would happen. John stepped forward to the judge and said, "I'm ready to accept any punishment, fine or imprisonment, but I don't think I or any man should be treated—insulted and degraded—this way because of color."

The judge agreed.

But this was not the last time that John had to defend himself with his fists, not just his words. When he learned that a white attorney was say-ing terrible things about him because of his color, he confronted the man, who pretended to deny what he said. John became enraged and kicked and slapped him. He entered the courtroom a few minutes later, along with the attorney with his bloody nose. The man complained that he had been assaulted by John and called him names in the courtroom. Again the judge agreed with John that he did not deserve to be treated that way. John felt that sometimes his dignity and honor needed to be defended by blows.

When court was in session, students were allowed to attend to listen and learn from his "strong, musical voice." So powerful were his speeches that people were known to weep.

Oberlin Street in 1860 when the Langstons lived in town. (Permission, Oberlin College Archives.)

He felt calmed when he returned to his home in the evenings to have dinner and long talks with his wife, and he played with little Arthur. Carrie listened and encouraged him to take advantage of new opportunities. He was elected to several positions over the next few years, including the Oberlin City Council and the town's board of education.

John and Carrie shared the joy of family life, while he remained actively involved in fighting for the freedom of slaves and the rights of black people. His activities frequently took him away from home. And true to their desires, they had two more sons and two daughters. They named them Ralph (b. 1857), Chinque (b. 1858, who died when she was two and a half), Nettie (b. 1861) and Frank (b. 1864). They also fostered children, including one from Africa, and boarded female college students.

Fugitive slaves, the ghost visitors he remembered from the plantation, often came to Oberlin seeking help and freedom. The Fugitive Slave Act of 1850 had made it impossible for runaway slaves to be safe, even when they reached free states such as Ohio. The slave-catchers prowled at night, sometimes in disguise, as they tried to catch the runaways in order to collect bounties.

Under the Fugitive Slave Act, the slave-catchers had the legal right to nab and return the runaways, but that didn't make it right, and abolitionists continued to help the fugitives. In 1857, matters became worse when the federal Supreme Court (mostly Southern justices on it) had ruled in the Dred Scott case that blacks were not citizens of the United States. Abolitionist Ohioans were rightly angry.

Oberlin was at the heart of a dramatic incident on September 13, 1858, when slave-catchers located and kidnapped John Price, a young runaway from Kentucky. He had been betrayed, for pay, by a white boy. Price had arrived in Oberlin two years earlier; nearly starving and dressed in ragged clothes. Like the other fugitives, Price was registered by John, who was the town clerk and John ordered that the "poor stranger" be given a stipend of $1.25 a week until he could find a job, which he did by working on a farm. Price and the other fugitives were well known and protected in the small Oberlin community.

John was out of town on business that September day. When he returned, the streets were strangely quiet, as if everyone had vanished. Then he learned what had happened. Slave-catchers, including a federal marshal, had followed through on their devious plan to snatch John Price. They bribed twelve-year-old Shakespeare Boynton for $10 to take Price for a ride in the country, where he would be grabbed before the Oberlin abolitionists could know what happened. Price called out for help when a buggy driven by an Oberlin student passed them, and the student sounded the alarm in town. Charles Langston, now a schoolteacher visiting from Chillicothe, immediately grabbed his loaded pistol and raced on horseback, along with 500 townspeople, students, and professors to rescue the terrified Price.

The chase group was outraged that Price had been snatched in broad daylight. They rushed by buggy, horseback, and on foot, for eight miles to the Wadsworth Hotel in Wellington where Price was being held. The slave-catchers were surprised that they had been found out and barricaded themselves in an upstairs room.

The angry crowd of Oberlinians and Wellingtonians shouted back and forth with the kidnappers. The kidnappers yelled that they were legally entitled to return Price to his owner. The rescuers were determined to save the man, but time was running out; the 5:00 P.M. train's whistle was sounding. Rescurers stormed inside the hotel, forced their way into the room where Price was held, and carried him away.

John Mercer Langston hurried after the rescue party, but he had gone fewer than five miles when he met one of the brave rescuers— bookseller Simeon Bushnell, who was returning in a speeding buggy with Price. Price looked pale as ashes and frightened. "Come on back, I have him," yelled Bushnell.

John waved but continued toward Wellington so he could hear the entire story from the rest of the men. Within minutes he saw Charles and Carrie's brother, Orindatus Simeon Bolivar Wall, who urged him to return with them. They were followed by townsmen, who were shouting, singing and rejoicing.

Price was hidden first with James Fitch, an active member of the underground railroad, then moved to the home of Professor James Fairchild, where he was concealed until he could be taken to Canada across nearby Lake Erie.

"A victory won in the name of Freedom," said Charles Henry Langston. The rescuers were greeted by more celebrations when they returned. In the gathering that followed, many, including John Mercer Langston, made powerful speeches against slavery and for freedom. The entire community solemnly pledged that no fugitive slave would ever be taken from Oberlin and made a slave again. John said the incident involving Price would never be forgotten in the history of Oberlin.

Later, the town held a Jubilee celebration, and John, again, was one of the impassioned speakers denouncing the evils of slavery. A newspaper covering the talk wrote, "No more eloquent speech was made yesterday than his."

That wasn't the end of the drama. A grand jury indicted thirty-seven members of the rescue group (white and black) for breaking federal law—a law now defended by pro-Southern President James Buchanan, who had been elected in 1856. Among them were Charles Henry Langston, O.S.B. Wall, and John Anthony Copeland Jr., who later played an heroic role at Harper's Ferry. Charles Henry was targeted for prosecution because he had been portrayed as the mob's leader, even though he had briefly tried to negotiate a peaceful settlement with the kidnappers.

Twenty-five of the men arrested were from Oberlin, and the rest were from Wellington. The authorities also wanted to arrest John Mercer

Langston, but they gave up when he proved that he was out of town when the rescue efforts began.

Some of the raiders outside the Cuyahoga County Jail in 1858. Charles Langston is in the center holding his hat (see detail at right). Carrie's brother, O.S.B. Wall, is second from left wearing a top hat. (Permission, Oberlin College Archives.)

Rather than post bond and remain free until their trials, the rescuers opted to stay in jail in Cleveland as a protest. They knew that a jury selected by Democrats in Cleveland would be prejudiced against abolitionists. So they decided to get attention for their antislavery cause by remaining imprisoned and speaking out in favor of the "higher law" than the Fugitive Slave Act. The higher law meant doing what was right. Supporting slavery was wrong.

Eighty-five days later most rescuers were released. However, Charles Langston and Simeon Bushnell were tried and found guilty. After Charles was convicted, he was allowed to speak. He spoke powerfully speak about liberty, justice, humanity, sound religious duties and the teachings of Christ.

Charles' defiant and eloquent remarks astonished the court and he ended up having to pay $100 fine (instead of $1,000) and spend another twenty days in prison (instead of six months). Bushnell's sentence was harsher. Charles, who had become a well-known abolitionist in the state by this time called for a "common humanity." He and Bushnell said they would continue breaking laws that were wrong. Charles reminded the court that his father was a Revolutionary War soldier, who had served under Lafayette. His father said that he had fought for his son's freedom as much as for his own.

John was one of the speakers at a large rally held to decide what to do next. A Cleveland newspaper wrote that he had trampled a copy of the Fugitive Slave Act. John urged everyone to hate the act not just because it enslaved black men, but because it also made prisoners of white men. "For God's sake, let us fall back up on our own natural rights and say to the prison walls 'come down,' and set these men at liberty." The crowd cheered.

On July 6, 1859, John was among the speakers at the town's Jubilee celebration. A reporter wrote, "He spoke fearless and startling words in opposition to the Fugitive Slave Act. . . . No more eloquent speech was made yesterday than his."

7

Recruiting the Troops

THE MOVEMENT TO ABOLISH SLAVERY was growing in strength and John was often visited by people with ideas on how to end the enslavement of blacks. One such visitor was a man who gave a false name at first, asking if he could walk home with John when he went for lunch. During their stroll down College Street, which was dappled by brightly colored fallen leaves, the man revealed his true identity and asked for secrecy. He was John Brown Jr., the son of the notorious abolitionist, John Brown, who was planning a raid on Harper's Ferry, West Virginia.

"It's a blow that shall shake and destroy American slavery itself," said the man quietly.

Brown wanted John to help him identify men to participate. The idea was to give the weapons to slaves so that they would rise up against their masters. They both knew that this could mean death for those involved in the attempt to capture the arsenal filled with weapons. Volunteers had to be willing to risk death for the cause. Even though he didn't plan to go with them, John helped recruit two heroic black men from Oberlin—Lewis Sheridan Leary and John Anthony Copeland Jr. Although they may have thought they were only rescuing slaves rather than capturing an arsenal, both men agreed to participate. Leary simply asked that his wife and child be taken care of if he should die. It was a promise that Charles Langston would personally keep.

On October 16, 1859, John Brown Sr. led the raid and captured the arsenal and several citizens of the town of Harper's Ferry. Colonel Robert E. Lee, then a Union officer, arrived to defend the U.S. armory. (Lee resigned from the Union army in April, 26, 1861, three days after his native state of Virginia seceded from the Union.) Lee's troops killed a number of raiders and captured others, including John Brown Sr., and Copeland. Both were tried, convicted and hanged. Leary was shot and killed during the initial battle.

John had hoped that slavery would be abolished when Abraham Lincoln, a Republican lawyer from Illinois, was elected president. However, southern states seceded from the Union long before Lincoln issued the Emancipation Proclamation on January 1, 1863. Anger over the call to abolish slavery was boiling over. The war of rebellion—the Civil War—was about to begin.

John shook his head when he read the latest news. "Sister Carrie, I must help with the war effort. The government needs more troops—hundreds of thousands. It has to be blacks, not just whites, who are fighting for the cause."

His wife pushed her breakfast plate aside. "But blacks aren't allowed to serve in white regiments."

John looked up from the newspaper and replied, "I've heard that several states will allow the

Abraham Lincoln was elected president in November 1860 on a platform of containing slavery—limiting its western spread. A month later, South Carolina was the first of eleven states to secede from the Union. The Civil War officially began in April 1861 when the Confederates fired the first shots at Fort Sumter. On January 1, 1863, President Lincoln issued the Emancipation Proclamation. The war did not end until 1865. Two-and-a half years later the last of the slaves learned that they were free. (public domain)

formation of black regiments, now that Congress will allow it."

"There's no one better than you to help rally troops," said Carrie.

"I'll be gone for a while," he said. "That's not going to be easy, especially for you."

"Go. The children and I'll be fine as always, Mercer," she responded. "We'll do what we can to help here."

John soon was working with George Stearns, a merchant from Boston, who had been a friend of John Brown. They met many times to discuss how they would recruit troops and what would be paid. John was also asked to address large assemblies.

He recruited blacks for the 54th Massachusetts Regiment by visiting Ohio, Indiana, and Illinois. There was no guarantee that the troops would survive battles. Because he had recruited them, John was heartbroken that the most of the first group to go into battle were killed in an attempt to take Fort Wagner in South Carolina.

One of the men who died there was the only child of an elderly woman who lived near Xenia, Ohio. After her son had been killed, the woman sought out John. He feared she was angry with him for recruiting her son. Instead, despite her great loss and sadness, the woman said that she hoped the cause would continue. "For liberty is better than life," she said.

"You are a worthy American mother," John replied.

After they had filled the ranks of the 54th Massachusetts Regiment, John's task was to find volunteers for the 55th. Most of the men enlisting were from Ohio. John was so proud of this group that he personally paid for having the colors—flags—made of the finest materials to be carried into battle. Carrie was among those at Oberlin who raised additional funds for flags.

John's success as a recruiter of black troops for Massachusetts led to a request by Ohio Governor David Tod for him to recruit a black regiment for Ohio. This was a change for Tod who had told John earlier that "to enlist a negro soldier would be to drive every white man out of the service. John insisted that the regiment be part of the national service, and eventually the 5th United States Colored Troops was formed. The troops mistakenly assumed they were going to be paid, just like soldiers who had joined the Massachusetts regiments,

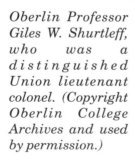

Oberlin Professor Giles W. Shurtleff, who was a distinguished Union lieutenant colonel. (Copyright Oberlin College Archives and used by permission.)

Illustration from John's autobiography of him presenting the colors to the 5th United States Colored Troops Camp Delaware, Ohio, page 210a.

but Ohio had no such plans. When the soldiers at Camp Delaware were told about the "mistake" they were also informed that they could simply go home, but none of the 300 men did. But because the state of Ohio had not planned to pay the men, John began raising money himself so that each man would have at least a small amount—$2.50.

Oberlin College Professor Giles W. Shurtleff, an abolitionist, was among the scholars asked to lead the troops because blacks were not allowed to be officers. John said that Shurtleff was "manly noble and brave," and was devoted to his troops.

John again had colors made for the regiment and his heart filled with pride when he, Ohio Governor Tod and others spoke to the soldiers. When it was John's turn he stood on a small platform next to the flag and fervently said to the regiment, "My boys, sons of the state, go forth now as you are called to fight for our country and its government." He urged them to be brave, intelligent and devoted. And he said, if their lives were spared in battle, he would greet them on his hands and knees when they returned. But if any were cowards, he would crawl away and never look in their faces again. The regiment led by Shurtleff served heroically in ten battles in Richmond and Petersburg, and won special distinction in New Market Heights.

In January 1864, John had a surprise encounter that would have amazed and probably amused Uncle Billy from the Louisa plantation. John had been asked by Tennessee Governor Andrew Johnson to address 10,000 black troops in a camp near Nashville and to thank them for their service on behalf of the government. Johnson had

Illustration from John's autobiography, titled "Addressing the colored troops at Nashville, Tenn., 1864," page 228a.

been a senator from the secessionist state, but was loyal to the Union. Lincoln appointed him as military governor in 1862.

It was quite a sight; the camp was packed with the soldiers. John climbed on a military wagon to use as a platform to address these heroes in the name of the president and the governor. He felt that anything he could say was tame and lifeless compared with their brave deeds. As he concluded his remarks, an elderly corporal with snow-white hair approached him. *He looks the perfection of a soldier,* John thought.

The man said, "John, how are you?"

"Do I know you?" responded John.

"Oh yes," replied the man in a fatherly manner. "For you did not weigh ten pounds when I held you in the hollow of this hand."

John was astonished. "You held me?"

"I knew your mother when she first came upon the Quarles plantation. I knew your half-brother William and his two sisters, and your brothers, Gideon and Charles."

John reached back in his memory. The man's words came from the "vasty deep." He wasn't able to remember him until there was a further explanation.

"What, sir, are you doing here?" He was surprised that a man as old as this was in the service.

"John, I have entered the service to fight until there is no more slavery in this land."

"You were never a slave," said John.

"Yes, always a slave, John, always a fugitive slave."

Major Dewey said to John, "That is the greatest man and the most influential of all the troops. His words inspirited and encouraged the men in the late great fight, making them firm, cool and reliable."

Indeed, the man was a fugitive slave, who had briefly terrified Uncle Billy at the Great House door. One of Uncle Billy's "ghosts" had become a fearless leader and hero in the battle for freedom.

With his recruiting duties finished, John returned to Washington, D.C., at his own expense, to try to talk the top military leaders into allowing black soldiers to advance into leadership positions. He had positive feedback during his meetings with the vice president and generals and thought his ideas would be implemented. But then General Robert E. Lee, now a Confederate leader, surrendered on April 9, 1865. With the Civil War now over, pressure for promoting black soldiers evaporated.

While John was in the nation's capital, the unthinkable happened—the "horror of horrors." President Lincoln, after his reelection to a second term, was assassinated five days after Lee surrendered to General Ulysess S. Grant at Appomattox Court House.

Just two nights earlier John had stood with a large crowd and listened to the thrilling words of the president. And now he was in the city that was shocked by the murder of the great man while his wife, Mary sat next to the president at Ford's Theater.

John heard the sad news from Vice President Andrew Johnson's black servant, Wade Hickman, who feared for Johnson's life in the hours following the shooting. Hickman assured John that he would not allow anyone to harm the vice president—the soon-to-be president.

How could anyone murder such a man? Lincoln was a statesman without equal. A grand leader, he was the savior of our country!

John remained in Washington to watch the funeral procession. A special honor was given to a black regiment. It was allowed to carry the coffin of the Great Emancipator from the hearse to the temporary resting place in the rotunda of the Capitol. John observed the sad and solemn procession along Pennsylvania Avenue. His heart filled with gratitude and pride as the regiment, representing the millions of his fellow countrymen, former slaves, whom the president had freed, processed.

John and a committee representing black people met with Johnson before he moved into the White House. John hoped that the new president would be like Lincoln. Johnson assured them he would not only uphold laws that had been enacted on behalf of blacks, but would also work on having an amendment to the Constitution introduced to eliminate slavery. However, Johnson did not act to unify the country as many had hoped.

8

The Aftermath of War

FREEDOM POSED ITS OWN PROBLEMS. Former slaves were suddenly on their own to find work, have homes, and to take care of their families. Southern whites were also struggling economically after the Civil War had destroyed farms, towns, factories, and transportation infrastructure. If they had owned slaves, now they had to hire workers, sometimes their former slaves. Other freed slaves migrated for new lives in the North. Under Lincoln's administration, funds had been appropriated for Reconstruction to help both blacks and whites recover from the war.

John decided to tour parts of the South to see how things were going for the newly freed even before the war ended. Against the advice of friends, he took the train to Louisville, Kentucky. Based on all the train robberies that had occurred, the journey could have been extremely dangerous. Trains had been attacked by both sides' forces during the war and by groups of lawless, and often illiterate, young men called "bushwackers." They had formed originally into small groups in Missouri. Bushwackers and other rebel groups still pushed trains from the tracks and robbed the passengers.

John decided to travel anyway, accompanied by William Howard, his brave black friend. They saw numerous wartime wrecks of trains alongside the tracks as they went from city to city, but arrived without problems in Louisville.

He observed freed slaves assisted by Northern charities and troops, and also communities that had been developed by free blacks before the war. That group of people was particularly helpful to the newly freed.

Once again he was glad to be home. The house on East College was filled with the sounds of small children, ranging in age from nine to newborn Frank. The Ralph raced to his arms and climbed in John's lap. Sweet Nettie wanted to sing for him and show him what she could play on the piano. Arthur begged to hear about his trip. The warmth of his family reminded him about the love he had felt from the Gooches and what he had been told by his brothers about life on the Louisa plantation.

When the house was finally quiet after the children were in bed, John and Carrie sat together near the parlor fireplace. He told Carrie about the inspirational people he had met and observed during his travels.

John stretched out his legs. "It's good to be home. When I see the homeless who are newly freed, starting to build shelter and attend churches and be educated as free men and women, I think about how blessed we are."

"I was impressed by the emancipated women I met," John continued. "They are practical and have good business sense. They're leaders and are helping the newly freed in all respects."

Carrie said, "I'm not surprised. We must do what we can to help them. Will you go back?"

"Yes," replied John. "It's still dangerous for many blacks. The Union army is protecting them during occupation. It will take a while for the rebel states to be able to fully return to the Union."

"I know they'll want you to talk," she said.

"At every opportunity, as slaves in each state become emancipated," he answered.

In early 1866, he was invited to visit St. Louis, Missouri, to speak at a celebration of emancipation. Freed blacks organized a large meeting at Veranda Hall, but so many people came that they removed all the chairs and everyone stood. The hall was packed, even though it cost $1 to attend.

John's oration was on the importance of education, labor, thrift, temperance, morality, and economy—all necessary for permanent progress in freedom. His words were greeted with outbursts of applause. His speech coincided with the state Constitutional Convention in Missouri that was meeting to consider civil rights for freed people in accordance with the U.S Constitution. Many were worried that those attending the convention would not adopt this important measure. John was invited to speak on behalf of the people of color. He gave a long oration, which was listened to patiently and without interruption. His words helped convince those voting at the convention to "provide for the colored people of the state their full measure of civil rights."

Because of his success in Missouri, John was asked to meet with the legislatures of other states; both whites and blacks turned out to hear him. In Kansas, he had a particularly thrilling welcome by the Republicans, the political party of Lincoln, and Republican newspapers had positive things to say about him. The papers owned by the Democrats were filled with what John told Carrie were "badly tempered, ill-advised and untruthful, disparaging comments on the whole affair."

"Other papers called you eloquent and praised you for telling our people to 'Get education!' 'Get money!' 'Get character.' And asked God's blessing on your work," she said.

"I appreciated one paper's response in my defense to an anonymous letter-writer who said I should get out of town. There have been threats of violence against me," John said. "But I will not be silenced. There's much to do."

9

Presidential Visit

AFTER TRIPS TO FOUR SOUTHERN STATES, John planned to stay home and resume his law practice. He enjoyed strolling around the college campus, and taking his children to Plum Creek, where they caught small fish and frogs. Or they wandered along the creek to watch the mills at work. They climbed favorite trees in the square and threw sticks for their white-and-tan hound named Louisa.

On walks about town, John pointed out where his professors lived, and where he attended classes in both the college and the seminary. The children especially enjoyed his stories about where he had met their mother, and how he had proposed to her. "And she said yes!" they shouted.

While he treasured his family moments, his law practice continued to thrive. Occasionally, he was asked to accept a tough case. At thirty-seven, John understood that we never know what would happen when we take on a new challenge.

An elderly man, and his daughter, who was not well, came to his office one day with an appeal for help. John told them to have a seat and asked how he could help. The young woman urged her despondent father to explain. The man cleared his throat and began. His only son had enlisted in the Union army in the early days of the war, and had served with honor and distinction. The young man had reenlisted, even though it was a burden on the family for him to be gone. "I needed him to help. I haven't been as well and strong as I once was," the old man said. "Besides, it was his patriotic duty— so we didn't complain."

But then, to their dismay, the young man had been influenced by other soldiers to go astray. Now he was in a military prison.

"Can anything be done?" the old man asked John. "Can you help him be released?" He wiped his eyes.

John listened carefully and reviewed all the letters and documents, which the man brought with him. He told them that he would see what he could do.

As John investigated, he learned that the soldier had never been in trouble before and had been well liked by his officers. However, the charges were serious. Apparently a number of soldiers in his regiment had been drinking and a man had been robbed.

Having met the commander-in-chief on other occasions, John decided to take the facts of the case directly to President Andrew Johnson for action.

John arrived in the capital in early 1867. As was the custom of the day, anyone who wanted to speak with the commander-in-chief would go to the executive mansion, the White House, and ask to be seen. It might take days or weeks.

Every day John and others heard the kind doorkeeper announce to those waiting that the president would not see anyone that day. "Come back tomorrow." But on a Saturday, he was told that the first opportunity might be on the following Tuesday. John was discouraged by the delays. He missed his work and his family.

On a Saturday, he asked again, and this time the acting doorkeeper, William Slade, recognized John as an old friend from Ohio. He agreed to

President Andrew Johnson, (1865–1869), was a Jacksonian Democrat from Tennessee, who supported states' rights.
(Photo courtesy of the National Park Service.)

bring his case immediately to the president's attention. John was led to the library. Two hours passed. Finally someone returned and said, "Be patient."

Then, Slade came to John and said, "Come now, Langston, the president will see you."

President Johnson greeted John warmly and listened to the case. He said, "I can't give this case immediate attention. There are thousands more like it before this one. I'll assign this to an officer to handle."

Then he allowed John a few more minutes to continue his appeal. John told him about the elderly father and the sick daughter. The president seemed moved by the additional details. "I'll see what I can do," said President Johnson. "Come back in three days."

The president and John differed politically on many issues. President Johnson was a native of North Carolina and had reflected Southern views when he served as a senator from Tennessee. The president had also favored the Fugitive Slave Act and had initially been opposed to the Emancipation Proclamation. After he became president upon the assassination of Lincoln, Johnson angered a number of people because he was lenient toward the South and had pardoned many Confederate soldiers. That did not mean that he couldn't be fair in this case. John left the White House feeling hopeful, but expecting that his appeal might take longer than the president had said.

Wrapped in a heavy coat, John walked around the streets of Washington, and past Ford's Theater where President Lincoln had been fatally shot not even a year earlier. Few people were out in the bitter January weather. He thought about Carrie and the children and hoped that they were warm enough. How much longer would he have to be away on this mission?

John was attending church the following day with the Slades when he received surprising news. As William Slade and other ushers passed the offering baskets to those in the pews, the White House doorkeeper whispered, "The president wants to see you now. Go at once."

Then Slade handed his basket to another usher and quickly explained to his family that he was leaving the service with John.

Not only was the president waiting for John, but so was General Ulysses S. Grant, the Secretary of War, who happened to be there to read a celebrated speech to the president.

"I'm on the mercy seat today," said President Johnson. "I've decided to take up your case and deal with it immediately."

John's heart quickened while the president continued. "Now, do you think that there is enough evidence to justify your petition?"

"Yes, sir," replied John, quickly.

"Well, then," said the president. "The papers will be signed for his release and reinstatement."

John couldn't wait to tell the soldier's family the good news.

But there was more to come from this visit to the nation's capital. President Johnson talked with John about politics and his law practice. He asked if he had been admitted to practice with the Supreme Court Bar. John shook his head. "No, sir."

The president then offered to write a letter of recommendation to Chief Justice Salmon P. Chase. John presented the letter the next morning to Justice Chase, someone he knew and respected from Ohio. Justice Chase was an abolitionist, whom John had supported when he ran for the Ohio Senate and later the governorship. Before he was appointed Chief Justice in June 1864, Chase ran unsuccessfully in 1860 for president. President Lincoln appointed him as head of the Treasury, and he was responsible for managing the finances of the Union during the Civil War. As such, he was instrumental in establishing the national banking system and issuing paper currency. Chase resigned his position in June 1864 and was appointed Chief Justice of the U.S. Supreme Court later that year. No wonder John was glad to see his friend again!

Mathew Brady portrait of Salmon P. Chase, former Ohio governor, Secretary of the Treasury, and later Chief Justice of the Supreme Court. (public domain)

Because there was a shortage of metal for civilian use during the Civil War, the federal government authorized Secretary of the Treasury Salmon Chase to issue "fractional currency" that was printed on paper in denominations of less than a dollar.

The five- and ten-cent pieces pictured were redeemable at any post office for stamps. This type of currency was issued in 1862. Then the later twenty-five cent bill was equal to a quarter. This currency was legal tender until 1876. In 1863 Secretary Salmon Chase advocated establishing a national banking system. The Chase bank is named for him.

A few days later, on January 17, 1867, John was admitted to the Supreme Court Bar, the first black attorney to have that distinction in the nation.

There was a second personal surprise. The Chief Justice suggested that John meet with General O. O. Howard, the commissioner of the newly formed Freedmen's Bureau. John was pleased when the general said he might need John's assistance with the bureau, but he replied that he had hoped to spend more time with his law practice because he had been away so much. He wanted to return to his work and family. He soon discovered that the nation demanded his services once again.

In April 1867, just as the redbuds flowered, and jack-in-the-pulpits bloomed along Plum Creek, several telegrams arrived in a single day urging him to return to Washington and meet with General Howard about serving with the Freedmen's Bureau. John didn't want to leave Oberlin for a distant job, no matter how many important people asked him.

It was Carrie who convinced him to learn more about what he was being asked to do before he made up his mind. Even though she and their friends encouraged him to go back to the capital, John still had misgivings. Yet he knew he had to answer his nation's call.

John turned sadly for one last look at his office, locked it and walked home down East College Street for his midday meal. He noticed how many more houses had been constructed since he

had started school there when he was just fourteen. Oberlin had swelled to more than 2,000
people. Almost one-fourth of the village's population was black, thanks to its reputation as a safe
and welcoming place for fugitive slaves, persons
of color, and abolitionists. Many newcomers had
settled in the village after the Civil War and their
homes were often larger than earlier ones.

John reached his white clapboard house. His
family had many questions: "Will you go?" "When
will you return?"

Looking at his children's faces, he was filled
with even more doubt and worry about what to
do, but he also recognized the importance of what
he was being asked. All he could manage to say
quietly was, "I think I will go."

John Mercer Langston, (1870s). Used by permission of the Oberlin College Archives.

Later, alone with Carrie, he admitted what was worrying him. While he was afraid that this new position would require him to give up his law practice, he had an even greater fear—that he would not be able to perform the new job well.

"I might fail," he said. "Everyone, including myself, will be disappointed in me."

"Mercer, Mercer," Carrie said pulling him into her arms. "You *will* not fail. I know you well. You *will* succeed. General Howard needs your assistance. Who better than you to help him?"

John knew she was right, but it didn't make it any easier to say good-bye. In a few days, he was back in Washington, meeting with General Howard. The general wasted no time in telling John what this would mean personally. "You will be appointed and commissioned as inspector general of the Bureau of Refugees, Freedmen and Abandoned Lands. This position will be difficult. It will tax all your abilities, including your eloquence, wisdom, discretion and self-sacrifice."

General. O. O. Howard, commissioner of the Freedmen's Bureau, and one of the founders of Howard University. (Photo by either Mathew Brady or Levin C. Handy, courtesy of the Library of Congress.)

John stood silently as the general continued. "You will inspire and encourage the freed people, especially in how to be self-sufficient. You need to continue to impress upon them the need for education for themselves and their children, and to be thrifty and save their money. You need to talk with them about how to deal with the prejudice and hate that they will encounter."

John nodded, and General Howard continued, "And, it is vital that you are careful not to provoke the ill will of those who were defeated in battle. Many of them were against emancipation and are still angry. That may be the most difficult challenge."

"Yes," said John. "Where will I serve?"

"The whole South," replied the general, "including the District of Columbia, Maryland, Kentucky, Tennessee and Missouri." He added that John would also visit the county of his birth.

John was further directed to contact all the Freedmen's Bureau officers in each area and to report on how they were doing in their jobs, especially in helping the freed slaves.

"Make sure you tell the freedmen to stay away from smoking tobacco," added the general. "It's expensive and not good for the body."

John nodded. There had been many crusades at Oberlin before and after the war about the use of liquor and tobacco, and even billiards.

"Now," said General Howard, standing up. "Mr. Langston, do you accept this mission? You may not say no, for this is your duty to your country and your race and to your Heavenly Father."

John said, "I accept the mission, with honor, General Howard."

"Good," was the reply. "Your pay will begin at once."

In the beginning, John commuted daily from Alexandria, Virginia, across the Potomac River, to the general's office. His tour of his southern district began with a trip to Maryland, then he went to Virginia, visiting Alexandria, Leesburg, Culpeper Courthouse, Orange Courthouse, Charlottesville, Gordonsville, Louisa Courthouse, then Richmond (the former Confederate capital), Petersburg and Fredericksburg.

Virginia, John thought. *I will be able to go back to Louisa at last.*

Many of these spots had been sites of fierce battles. Whites were still angry in the states that had left the Union. The war had ended, but people's emotions and hearts had not healed. John's duties were to examine the schools of the freed people and to examine and speak to the students. He also was expected to represent the Republican party and its doctrines and to encourage blacks to register to vote Republican. As General Howard had hinted, John's acceptance as a black person traveling in these southern regions to perform this work would not be easy in all situations.

10

Louisa Homecoming

BEFORE JOHN COULD VISIT LOUISA Courthouse, there were other stops to make in Virginia. His thoughts were increasingly on the place where he was born and on visiting his parents' graves. He wondered if Ralph and Lucy were still remembered thirty-three years after their deaths.

He had work to do before his arrival by train at the Louisa station. That involved checking on the activities of the Freedmen's Bureau in several communities, and participating at gatherings with local Republicans. He often spoke at meetings about the need for the party's ongoing support for the newly emancipated and their friends. It was the party of Lincoln, after all—the party that had been most helpful and welcoming to the blacks before and after the war.

One of those occasions was in Leesburg in Northern Virginia, not far from Washington, D.C.

On June 2, 1867, John, accompanied by William Downey, Generals Farnsworth and Pierce, and

Colonel L. Dudley, left Washington for the forty-mile train ride along the Potomac River to Leesburg in the foothills of the Blue Ridge Mountains. The orchards were in bloom and hay was ready for a first cut. Thickets of wild blackberry bushes cloaked in fading clusters of white flowers grew along the tracks. John leaned out the coach window and remembered the fragrance of the crops and the rich earth.

A meeting was scheduled at the Republican-owned hotel in Leesburg and lunch for the group was set for one P.M. The hotel's landlord barred John at the dining room door, saying that he could not enter.

John was shocked. He had not expected to be greeted this way! General Farnsworth noticed what was happening and immediately asked, "What's the matter?"

The landlord pointed at John and replied emphatically, "This man wants to go in the dining room and take his dinner at my first table with my white boarders. He shall not do it."

The general said equally emphatically, "Yes he will, and we will stand by him!"

Colonel Dudley said he agreed with the general.

John said, "Mr. Landlord, I shall eat dinner with my friends."

The landlord was adamant. "You don't understand. If I let you go in and eat now, my hotel and all the property I own will be burned. Please, sir, let me arrange to have you eat in your room. My waiters will take care of you."

John was dismayed that a hotel might be burned just because he, a black person, might eat with his friends in its dining room. He asked, "Mr. Landlord, will they really burn your hotel?"

The landlord, with a fearful look said, "Yes."

John said, "Then you may arrange my dinner in my room and Colonel Dudley will eat there with me."

The landlord hurried off to tell his staff. He was relieved that the situation had been resolved.

Despite the confrontation, the meetings and speeches went well in Leesburg, and later that evening John and his friends took a carriage along the banks of Goose Creek to stay in the little Quaker town of Hamilton, about six miles away, where they were warmly welcomed. For fun the next morning before breakfast, they took a horse-back ride across part of the mountains, then returned for breakfast and a meeting in a beautiful grove. Those attending were gracious and enjoyed the speakers, and the picnic luncheon.

John and his group returned to Leesburg where they would board a train for the return trip. They had a few hours to wait for its arrival, so they decided to have supper at the same hotel. However, the situation was now worse. They were denied entry to the building itself, not just the dining room, because John's companions were the same group of white men who had insisted on eating with him, a black man, the day before.

"I don't believe it," said Colonel Dudley. "Let's go to the hotel across the street. I know it's owned by a Democrat and former rebel, but perhaps he will let us sup."

Instead of turning them away, this man received them kindly, even after he looked at the register where they had signed their names. John had boldly written: *John Mercer Langston, Negro, Oberlin, Lorain County, Ohio.* He had made it abundantly clear who he was.

The first hotel, which had turned them away burned to the ground shortly thereafter, perhaps by those who were angry that John and his friends had been allowed to stay there even though they had been rejected the second time.

John later told his wife, "The Republican landlord lost more than he had gained by his illegal and unseemly conduct. He sowed the wind and reaped the whirlwind."

And he added that the owner of the other hotel, had been kind "to a colored wayfarer, who, tired, worn and hungry, knocked at the door of his house and became the popular one of the town." That hotel's business greatly improved, he said.

Finally, on June 15, 1867, John arrived in Louisa Courthouse on the midday train from Gordonsville, a rail junction, where he had spoken the day before. The Freedmen's Bureau was located in the once elegant Exchange Hotel in Gordonsville, which had been used as a hospital for the newly freed after the war. Earlier, the building conveniently located near the station, was used as a receiving hospital during the Civil War.

The Exchange Hotel in Gordsonville (now a Civil War museum) is next to the train station at the junction of the Orange Alexandria Railroad and the Central Virginia, and stagecoach routes. During the Civil War it was used as a receiving hospital for 70,000 Confederate and Union troops and during Reconstruction it was Union-occupied as the Freedmen's Bureau from 1867–1868. There were 200 black adults and fifty black children registered to read and write in the building. A replica classroom features an original wooden desk. (author photos)

The Gordonsville train station in 2016, about to undergo restoration. The working tracks are near the historic "exchange," where passengers changed trains to continue their journeys. (author photo)

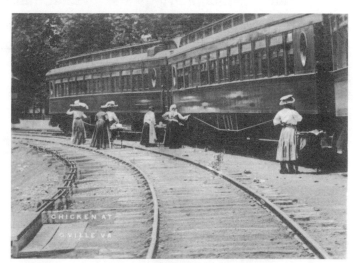

Beginning in 1854, slaves treated waiting passengers to fried chicken, sandwiches and fruit. After the war, the fried chicken vendors started their own business and charged for the meals. Gordonsville became famous for its fried chicken. Their food service came long before trains provided food and beverages on board. (Photo, courtesy of the Exchange Hotel Civil War Museum.)

John was eager to try the fried chicken lunch, cooked by black women known as waiter-carriers and sold to passengers through the train's windows during the Gordonsville stop. The women had begun serving passengers before the Civil War, and after being freed, they sold food to earn money. Although the town became most famous for the fried chicken, the women also served pies, cakes, boiled eggs, strawberries and cream, other fruit, tea and coffee, biscuits, sandwiches, ham and eggs.

The southeast-bound train, puffing white smoke from its wood-burning engine, passed through farmland, and traveled by plantation homes, before stopping briefly at Trevilian Station, a flag stop about five miles outside of Louisa.

While the train paused to take on a sack of mail, one of the passengers said to John, "Sir, look over there. On the small porch of that house is where Custer had his field office for a day or so during the battle of Trevillians."

Front porch where Custer set up his field office near Trevilian Station in June 1864. (author photo)

"Largest cavalry battle of the

war," said another, shaking his head. "Destroyed the tracks. Dead men and horses were everywhere."

John wiped the perspiration off his forehead and peered out for a glance at the white frame house near the tracks. He knew of the battle, which had occurred just three years earlier. It was close to his plantation birthplace, located only a few miles to the northeast.

The train squealed and started again. John stared out the window as the tracks crossed the road to Kent's Mill, and then passed over another dirt road that led to his father's former plantation. After rounding a bend, the town was in sight. It was a short walk from the Louisa depot to the hotel on Main Street, almost across from the courthouse building where he was to give his oration.

He wiped his brow again, straightened his jacket and put on his hat. As he stepped off the train, John was filled with excitement at returning "home"

Louisa depot. (Courtesy Louisa County Historical Society)

after more than three decades. He had no distinct memories of the town, although his brothers had told him what they recalled.

A crowd of 1,500—including 500 members of a club called the Union League—greeted John at the station. The secret Union League clubs of mostly black men had formed after the war to help register male black voters and to encourage them to vote Republican. They also discussed political and civic issues. When John appeared, the crowd divided into two sections of 750 each. Captain McCraken, the club's white president took John by the arm and walked with him between the sections down the street to the hotel where he would be staying. It was quite a procession. The crowd had come from all over and so the side streets were filled with buggies, wagons, mules and horses.

As John was about to enter the hotel he saw that the crowd had swelled and that many whites had come to hear him. He hoped that the stop in Louisa would be friendly and without problems.

It was then that he noticed "a large, fine looking, intelligent and influential man, apparently white, who seemed to be greatly angered at what was taking place." *What was going on?* John wondered if there would be trouble.

"Who is he?" John asked Captain McCracken, who was among the men escorting him to his room.

"Oh, that's William Fitzhugh Gordon Jr. He's the commonwealth attorney here, and the meanest rebel in the county. We call him general."

"He looks like he's angry at me," said John, anxiously.

"Yes," said the captain. "He's mad because we are having this meeting and you are to address us. He would break it up if he could. But thank God he cannot do so."

"Should I be worried?" asked John as the door of his room swung open and the captain placed his bags inside.

"No. The whole county has come to see you. They remember you as the Quarles boy and Lucy's son. We don't expect a disturbance."

The original Louisa County Court House, 1818, was located in front of where today's large brick building stands. (Courtesy Louisa County Historical Society)

John looked around his simple room after his friends left. He pulled the lace curtain aside and peeked out at the waiting crowd. Many waved fans to keep cool, or sat in the shade near the courthouse across the street.

He heard someone enter the room without knocking. It was a young white man, who said, "Are you one of us?"

"What do you mean?" asked John, a bit surprised and slightly alarmed.

"Are you one of us?" the young man repeated, without introducing himself.

John hesitated. He didn't have any idea what the man was getting at. He finally said, "Excuse me for not understanding you, but please explain yourself."

The young man said, "Are you a Virginian? Were you born in Louisa County?"

John relaxed and replied, "Yes, to your questions. And, in fact, my parents are both buried near here. The records of my birth and family are in the courthouse, and I am very interested in everything that pertains to this county and the Commonwealth of Virginia."

The young man smiled and responded, "Then I invite you to speak from my porch. All distinguished Virginians speak from it."

Before John could reply, Captain McCracken returned and officially introduced John to the young man, who was in fact, the hotel's owner. When the man repeated his invitation for the use of the porch, arrangements were quickly made for John to speak there rather than on the courthouse steps.

John stepped outside the hotel for his two P.M. oration. He was amazed at the size of the crowd, both blacks and whites, waiting for him in the heat. Everyone seemed glad to see him, except for General Gordon, who still looked full of spite and anger. He was standing at the far right of the audience. John focused on the community's warm welcome, instead of the general's sullen gaze.

The crowd quieted as John began his speech. He talked about his parents, and their resting place, side by side on a plantation where they had lived for so many years. He mentioned his father's executors, including Nathanial Mills, William Gooch and his father's nephews David Thompson and John Quarles, who had taken care of his father's estate and made sure that his desire to free slaves and take care of bequests were managed.

"And many years have passed. The great war has ground the shackles of the enslaved to dust, and all are free, white and black, uniting in a common purpose to make the country great, prosperous and happy. I rejoice to stand before you, in the county of my birth."

After fifteen minutes of introductory remarks, John was about to begin his prepared speech when he noticed that General Gordon had moved closer. He was now seated on the porch near the other influential men from the community. The general settled into his chair, fixing his eyes on him. John's oration lasted two and one half hours, and the general gave John's words his full attention, as did everyone else listening that steamy June day.

When John finished, General Gordon stood up and to his surprise, extended his hand. He said, "Langston, you are one of us and we are proud of you."

John could hardly believe his ears. He had little time to think about what had just occurred, as the huge crowd quickly swarmed the porch. Everyone wanted to thank John and touch him. Many of the elderly blacks, "burdened with cares and many broken by the tasks of their former lives," said, "I knew your father, John." "God bless you." "I knew your mother." "I never thought I would see this day."

Illustration from John's autobiography (page 270a) titled "After the speech at Louisa Court House, Virginia, 1867."

After some time, John became exhausted by all this kind attention and he asked a friend if he could go back to his room to rest. As he left the porch with Captain McCracken, he was surprised to find General Gordon heading upstairs with them to his room. What's more, the general adjusted the pillows on his bed.

The general turned to John and said, "Before you go to sleep, let me beg your pardon for the many blasphemous, vulgar expressions which I have made against you and against your coming here to address our people. I trust you will forgive me. I personally want to welcome you to this community. We are all proud of you and your wonderful speech."

John was filled with wonder and delight at the total change in a former enemy. It was certainly not what he had expected when he had seen the general's face earlier that day. But it was not the end of surprises from the man.

While John was dining at Captain McCracken's house that evening, General Gordon appeared at the front door and insisted that John speak to a club of white ladies the following night at a Baptist church. John's friends objected, fearing that there might be trouble. The general insisted that there would be no problems because not only did the women want to hear John, the general himself would be in charge.

It turned out to be a memorable event. John spoke to them on the topic of "The duty of the

American woman in this hour of reconstruction."
When he was finished, he received flattering comments, and all the ladies shook his hand.

As he headed back to the hotel, the general surprised him yet again by inviting John to join him for breakfast the next morning. John remembered the treatment he had received at the first hotel in Leesburg and did not want to be embarrassed again. He told the general that he would only join him if they were to dine as equals.

At seven A.M., John and his friends met the general and his wife at a table in the hotel dining room. Because it was the first time that someone of "Negro extraction" had been allowed to eat in that place, a lot of people in the community talked about it for days, mostly favorably, John later learned.

After breakfast, John, along with many Virginia friends and relatives, went by carriage and horse to the William Kent plantation (originally part of his father's land), three miles from the courthouse, to visit his parents' graves. John knelt to touch the weed- and vine-covered stones under a large tree. The crowd was silent while he thought about his father and mother, who had cared so much about him and his future.

Family friends then shared stories of Ralph and Lucy, especially her devotion to her children, and worries about what would happen to little John.

Illustration from John's autobiography on page 272a shows him standing over his parents's graves near Kent's Mill. The illustrator uses a weeping willow to capture the emotion of the moment.

Stones still mark the outlines of the graves of Ralph Quarles and Lucy Langston at a corner of what was once Ralph's vast plantation. The foundation of a small house nearby is possibly where their daughter Maria Powell lived with her family. (Photo courtesy of the Louisa County Historical Society)

11

The Gift of Oratory

A S JOHN HAD FEARED when he took the position of inspector general of the Freedmen's Bureau, his travels took him away from Carrie and the children for lengthy periods. After his official tour of Virginia, he made an extended trip through Mississippi and Alabama. In reading the newspapers, John learned that President Johnson was considering making changes in the bureau's leadership and that his name was under consideration as a replacement for John's boss, General Howard.

Johnson called John to the White House and spoke harshly about Howard's management as commissioner. He asked if John were willing to take the position. John replied, "Mr. Howard was appointed by President Lincoln, and he seems very wise and efficient. He's serving the black community well. He's also respected by the people who run charities to help the formerly enslaved."

President Johnson could see that John was serious about not replacing General Howard, so he asked him to consider becoming minister to Haiti. John again said no. He wasn't interested in serving in a foreign land at that time.

"Think it over," said the president, "and we can talk again in a few days."

John had other thoughts. He was alarmed that the president would replace a man who had done such a good job. He decided to warn General Howard about what the president had said. After their talk, John spoke with others who agreed to help, including Colonel L. Edwin Dudley, and John T. Johnson, a prominent black man, who was also a friend of General Howard. They decided to take their concerns to General Ulysses S. Grant, who was still Secretary of War.

Grant listened attentively. He said he would try to help keep Howard from being fired, but shook his head about President Johnson. "I have no influence with him. His reasons are personal, political and partisan." Grant went on to say how much he agreed with John and the others, especially ensuring that blacks would be allowed to vote. "They deserve full citizenship," said Grant.

"You deserve to be president," John said. "I would nominate you if I could in the name of blacks everywhere."

Later, the well-liked General Grant was elected president in 1868. Johnson had been impeached, but not convicted, earlier that year. Probably thanks to General Grant, General Howard was not replaced as commission of the bureau.

During the two and a half years that John worked for the bureau, he made numerous visits to the former slave-holding states. What he found in North Carolina particularly pleased him. The former slaves were making strides in education

General Ulysses S. Grant led the Union armies to victory and later became the eighteenth U.S. president. A Radical Republican, he worked to implement Congressional Reconstruction and eliminate the vestiges of slavery. (Photo circa 1875. Mathew Brady or Levin C. Handy. Public domain.)

and jobs. Education was valued, and churches had large congregations. Plus he was a sought-after and highly praised orator. In 1867, the Raleigh *Weekly Standard* covered his oration that focused on education. The newspaper said that for almost two hours John had kept the audience "spellbound by his genius and eloquence." On November 5, 1867, he made a second visit to Raleigh. The *Weekly Standard* again wrote about his one-hour speech on Republican principles. The paper called it eloquent and the best they had ever heard.

His travels also took him to Fort Sumter, South Carolina, where the first shot of the rebellion had been fired. It was a beautiful day along the coast.

Later that moonlit evening, a huge crowd—it seemed like the entire city of Charleston, whites and blacks—had turned out at the Battery within sight of the fort. His speech was about education, property and devotion to the government by the formerly enslaved, and the reconciliation and happiness of white former masters. John finished his two-hour oration to deafening applause. He left feeling very optimistic for the future of all peoples.

John continued on to Louisiana where another paper, the New Orleans *Republican* cheered his arrival and said, in advance of his talk on New Year's Day, 1868, "No worthier man has stood upon its platform, no abler man has reasoned with people who are there to assemble. Go early and you will need no further inducement to remain late."

In order to return to the Union, the Confederate states that had seceded had to ratify new amendments to the Constitution and incorporate these laws in the state constitutions. The 14th Amendment offered equal protection under the law to males, and the 15th Amendment gave the right to vote to black men. John would help the process around the South.

While John toured schools and met with people in the area, he was honored that leading men from the state Constitutional Convention, which was meeting in New Orleans, came to hear him. He was described by newspapers as a wise and influential statesman. The New Orleans *Republican* newspaper said of John's talk on January 1, that he spoke on the single topic of how blacks had always been citizens of the United States. He maintained that the Constitution of the United States made no distinction of color or race. This was a major theme of his orations. The paper also noted that John sometimes used wit and sarcasm that swayed the audience "as if by the hand of an enchanter. Many applauded in spite of themselves."

While in Louisiana, John helped influence a change in the state constitution that lowered the age for candidates for governor and lieutenant governor from thirty to twenty-five. And he spent hours persuading Oscar J. Dunn, a black man, to run for lieutenant governor. Dunn had misgivings. Dunn and John walked up and down Canal Street in the middle of the night, and finally returned home where John urged him to run—this time in front of Dunn's wife. After listening to John she said, "My husband, you must do your duty."

Dunn ran and won—the first black to be elected to such an office in the nation.

John continued on to warm receptions in Alabama, and then Georgia, where he visited black schools and lobbied for better student materials.

He still encountered prejudice and resistance, however, such as when in Albany, Georgia, he urged the young black men in the audience to become educated and even serve in high national offices.

"Never! Never, in the United States of America!" shouted an elderly white man seated on the stage near John. But it wasn't long after that when John's prediction came true. In 1870, Jefferson Long, a black man, was elected to Congress from the Macon, Georgia, district.

For all the speeches and newspaper reports of his talks, nothing seemed to make John more proud than his work with young people. During his visits to schools, he wanted to inspire parents and children to become educated so they could advance in life. He encouraged teachers and principals in their work. He had learned early on in his own life that education was critical to success.

And he was impressed by the number of Northern whites who had come to the South, often as volunteers, to help educate and improve the lives of the former slaves.

Through his work with Freedmen's Bureau, John promoted schools and learning wherever he went. It was no wonder that he would be asked to do even more in the field of education.

~ ~ ~

John now had an even greater new opportunity. Howard University was founded in 1867 and named for its founder General Oliver Otis Howard.

The university administration wanted to open a law school for men and women, blacks and white. For many reasons John was a logical choice to develop that new department. The trustees said John was ineligible to be a professor according to the bylaws because he wasn't a member in good standing of an evangelical church. But, because the trustees wanted him, they changed the rule, and on October 12, 1868, John began establishing the law department and was named its first dean, a position he held for seven years.

John knew from experience how important it was for lawyers to give excellent impromptu speeches and to master the skills of debate. They needed to be effective speakers. He required "moot courts" in which the students would manage all aspects of a real court. The law school hired instructors who could keep the attention of the most indifferent students. Students would learn to debate both sides of an issue to sharpen their skills. John set up a schedule that allowed law students to work during the day, often for President Grant or his cabinet, and then attend their classes beginning at five P.M. to accommodate John's work schedule.

On Sunday mornings, the students were required to attend lectures on professional ethics. The first class consisted of ten students, one woman and nine men. After three years of instruction and practicing what it was like to be in court, the students took their examinations and were admitted to practice before the Supreme Court.

While he was dean, John spotted Ralph Waldo Emerson, the famed American essayist, lecturer, and poet, at breakfast one Saturday. John quickly took advantage of the moment and invited Emerson to speak the following morning, on January 7, 1872, during the scheduled lecture time.

Emerson agreed and talked about ideas and active minds before giving the students a list of books that they should read. The books included those written by Edmund Burke, Boswell, Goethe, and Shakespeare. Emerson said, "The greatest minds value Shakespeare the most."

When Emerson finished, John told the students that this had been a rare moment, and that if word had gotten out about this speaker, the campus would have been swarmed by people wanting to hear him.

Emerson's lecture brought national and world fame to the university. His words were sent out "on the wings of the wind to the uttermost parts of creation." His address even appeared in the *New York Times* the following Monday. He told the students that he had hesitated to speak at first because it was not usually his habit to speak without careful preparation. But he showed through his talk that he was a "master of himself and his thoughts." John told Carrie later that he thought that Emerson's address had far greater influence for the good of the students than any others.

Howard's law school continued to thrive, and eventually there were more than 100 students. President Grant was supportive of the school, and especially its black students. John was proud when the first class of black law students ever known in the United States were graduated from Howard, and also the law school's first woman, Charlotte B. Ray, graduated with high honors.

Charles Sumner, an American politician and senator from Massachusetts, canceled his speaking engagement at Columbia Law School to give the oration at Howard that first commencement.

American essayist, lecturer and poet Ralph Waldo Emerson. His most famous work is Self-Reliance. *He describes a self-reliant man as someone who is not afraid to speak his mind and truth to anyone. (S. A. Schoff engraving, courtesy of the Library of Congress.)*

John prided himself on his relationships with his students. He was considered a parent and benefactor. Those days with the students were the happiest of his professional life, especially when he could hand diplomas to the black students, many of whose families had come out of slavery.

In 1873, President O. O. Howard announced his plans to retire. The trustees honored John by appointing him to serve as acting president, and vice president of the board of trustees for an annual salary of $1,500. He would manage the entire university while running the law school. Although he had concerns about his ability to take on this role, General Howard assured him that he would do fine. And John did. Enrollment increased and the university grew in favor, and indigent students were assisted financially.

During commencement exercises, the school had a surprise for John. General Howard returned, interrupted the ceremony, and conferred a Doctor of Law degree on John.

After two years of running the school, John decided it was time to move on. The university needed to hire a full-time president. The position hadn't been offered to him, so he resigned in June 1876.

12

Health and Banking Duties

John was a man who couldn't refuse multiple responsibilities. While he served as dean of Howard Law School, President Grant appointed him on March 15, 1871, to the Board of Health for the District of Columbia because of his legal skills. It was a prestigious position and John would be the first black board member. The five-member board had been established by Congress and each member received a salary of $3,000 per year. Other board members included Drs. Christopher C. Cox, and D. Willard Bliss (allopathic medicine), and T. S. Verdi (homœpathic medicine). The fifth member was businessman John Marbury Jr. of Georgetown, who served as the board's treasurer.

Like most cities of the time, Washington, D.C., had health issues partly caused by domestic and work animals running loose. Animals defecated in the streets. Dead animals were often left in the roads, causing additional health problems. There were other problems that caused diseases, such as garbage and human waste. Sanitation ordinances were needed to clean up the streets. John's job would be to write them once the board decided what it wanted to regulate. At the first meeting, perhaps as an oversight, John was the only member who was not introduced by District of Columbia Governor H. D. Cooke. In fact, the governor had asked all the others about what suggestions or questions they might have and was about to adjourn the meeting when John spoke up.

He soon demonstrated that he was the only one fully prepared for his duties. Before the meeting, he had located and read sanitary reports and learned about how the boards of health in other

"Board of Health of the District of Columbia." Illustration, page 318a from John's autobiography. John is pictured in the center. Clockwise from top left, Bliss, Marbury, Cox and Verdi.

states were operating. The other board members were impressed by his knowledge and the information he shared.

Among his responsibilities he was put in charge of the Committee on Ordinances, and became the attorney for the board's committee, which met weekly. They listened to the business community and had public meetings where there was free and open debate.

There were numerous issues to consider besides animals. They looked at products, such as vegetables, animals or fish that might be unfit for consumption. In each instance, they tried to balance the rights of the owners of animals roaming the streets of Washington and nearby Georgetown with the public's health. The board was concerned about the spread of diseases, such as smallpox, yellow fever, typhoid, and other contagious diseases. Drainage was an problem, as well as garbage disposal. The board's reports were published in the local press.

As part of his duties, John went on the road to study the programs being implemented in Baltimore, Philadelphia, New York, and Boston and then to report back to the committee.

On a visit to New York with Dr. Bliss, he again showed a sense of humor about his complexion, just as he had done in Brownhelm. Dr. Bliss, a white man, had skin that was darker than John's. When they met with the New York Board of Health, member Alfonzo Boardman said he had heard that they had a black man on their board. John quickly answered, "Yes, we have. He is a man of great ability." In glowing terms John continued to describe the talents of such a man, while Dr. Bliss listened and wondered what John was up to. He was afraid John would make a fool of himself. John then introduced Dr. Bliss as the black member of the board.

Bliss continued with the ruse by saying that it was true that there was a black man present, "but it hasn't yet been determined whether my friend Langston, or myself is that person."

There was much laughter in the room, John later told Carrie. But he had made a point to others about not making assumptions about people based on the color of their skin.

The ordinances that John wrote for the board were adopted and used as a model for other cities, including the nation of Japan.

John faithfully served this board for six years while at the same time fulfilling his obligations as

Dr. Williard Bliss, who later served as the chief surgeon for President James Garfield. (Matthew Brady, photographer, c. 1865, public domain.)

a professor and acting president at Howard University.

When he resigned from the Board of Health, members presented him with a beautiful gold ring with rare cameo settings. The faces on the cameo were of Minerva and Mars. Minerva was the Roman goddess of wisdom, medicine, commerce, handicrafts, poetry, the arts, and war. Mars was the Roman god of War.

~ ~ ~

John played a role in other events of the time. One such event was the funding and erection of the first memorial to Lincoln, a large bronze monument that had been the idea of Charlotte Scott, a freed slave from Virginia, who was now living in Marietta, Ohio.

When Charlotte Scott heard the terrible news of Lincoln's assassination in April 1865, she gave the first $5 she had earned as a freed slave to her employer. She asked him to find someone with influence to design the memorial.

Her generosity spurred a fund-raising campaign; it reached the attention of James E. Yeatman and the Western Sanitary Commission of Missouri. John heard about her idea through that group. He told freed people of the South about Scott's idea and the need for funding. The black troops, still in service, were especially interested and gave generously. The government had provided $3,000 for the foundation and a ten-foot-high granite pedestal. By April 1876, the $17,000 monument was ready to be unveiled in Washington, D.C.

Congress declared the day of the unveiling as a national holiday. More than 100,000 people attended, including President Grant and cabinet members.

John, as the presiding officer of the event, was scheduled to receive the work on behalf of the emancipated. But when he saw that President Grant was seated near the covered statue, he asked Grant to pull the cord to remove the cloth covering.

The audience roared with appreciation, cannons were fired and patriotic music was played. It was a moment of great rejoicing and enthusiasm. John described the statue as follows: "The martyred president, in bronze, stands beside a monolith upon which is a bust of Washington in bas relief. In his right hand he holds the Proclamation while his left is stretched over a slave upon whom his arms are bent, who is just rising, and from whose limbs shackles have just burst. The figure of the slave is that of a man worn by toil, with muscles hardened and rigid. He is represented as just rising from the earth, while his face is lighted with joy as he anticipates the full manhood of freedom. Upon the base of the monument is cut the word 'Emancipation.'"

Some blacks, including Frederick Douglass, disapproved of the statue because it was designed by a white artist, Thomas Ball, and depicted a black man submissively on his knees. Others, including John, believed the statue honored Lincoln for emancipating the slaves and raising them out of bondage.

Frederick Douglass was among the participants and gave an oration. His speech was a critical appraisal of Lincoln, a white man, with a white man's prejudices, who opposed slavery, but delayed taking action to free them after he was elected.

During the speeches, Yeatman said that honor and glory should be given to Charlotte Scott, whose "offering of gratitude and love, like that of the widow's mite, will be remembered in heaven."

Emancipation statue in Lincoln Park near Capitol Hill. At the unveiling ceremony in 1876 orator Frederick Douglass said the statue "showed the Negro on his knee when a more manly attitude would have been indicative of freedom." (public domain)

~ ~ ~

In addition to his other responsibilities during this time, in 1872 John served on the board of the Freedman's Savings and Trust Company, which had branches all over the South. Chartered in 1865, and run by whites, it was a place where black Union soldiers and the newly freed could make deposits in safety and could also be hired to learn how to work for banks. During his travels, John often spoke to groups about this bank and urged people to become its customers. Eventually, blacks deposited more than $3 million.

In 1872, when John became a member of the bank's finance committee, he learned that funds had been manipulated, and money that was deposited had been used for other purposes, such as bad loans. Although the bank initially had acted responsibly, now the money wasn't there, as customers discovered when they rushed to withdraw their savings. There were significant losses; John resolved to make changes in an attempt to save the bank. As time went on, John objected to two "unfortunate" things that happened.

In March 1874, Frederick Douglass, a board member for several years, was elected as bank president to take over from John W. Alvord, the bank's founder and president. John was opposed to Douglass' appointment because he thought he would find the position "difficult, trying and disappointing." Others hoped that Douglass, who had invested personally, could provide the leadership needed to save the bank. John does not mention that Douglas had been talked into investing and lost about $10,000 before the bank folded.

John's concern about Douglass' ability to turn the bank around when it was failing was perhaps warranted. After a few days in office, Douglass said that friends who persuaded him to take the position had "married him to a corpse."

The second issue was the trustees' decision to close the bank in June 1884. John was opposed to its closure and how the assets were to be divided. More than 60,000 people, who had deposited their savings, lost millions. John thought the depositors should have received more than they did.

These and other disagreements with Douglass would be factors later when John ran for Congress.

13

Presidential appointment to Haiti

JOHN CONTINUED HIS ACTIVITIES with the Republican Party and, prior to the nominating convention of 1875, campaigned for James Blaine for president. When that campaign faltered, John supported Rutherford B. Hayes, then-governor of Ohio. After Hayes won the election, John was considered for, and appointed to, one of five foreign-service appointments. He would serve as resident minister in Haiti.

He realized that the information about the duties provided by the State Department was inadequate. Although he felt he could deal with international law, he wasn't fluent in French, the language of the country. However, in his youth he had studied the history of the island and admired its heroes.

Like his other projects, he began learning all he could about this new appointment, including its government and special character, its history, its slavery and dictators. Despite frequent revolutions, during the past seventy years, its people "had maintained their nationality and independence." Haitians were emancipated under Touissant Louverture, nicknamed "Black Spartacus," and established sovereignty from France under Jean-Jacques Dessalines.

Many of the country's leading men were scholarly and accomplished in medicine, law and business. Children were educated in schools mostly run with government funding by the Roman Catholic Church. John was impressed that Haiti was such a progressive nation, despite its history of political instabilities, and he also knew that this country, run by blacks, was what he had dreamed of in his youth. Now he would live there as the diplomatic and consular representative of the United States.

On September 28, 1877, a few months after his appointment, he left New York City on the steamer *Andes* of the English Atlas Steamship Company. It was his first ocean voyage; the rough seas caused him to be seasick for three days. By the time the ship reached land, he was feeling much better. The *Andes* was greeted by a pilot to guide it into port. Soon after anchoring, officials arrived in small boats. John had never seen men of such dark complexions holding such high positions. They climbed aboard, using a rope ladder, and spoke with both the British captain and John.

The captain said that he would show John the sights in "Cape Haytian" before he dropped him off in the island's capital Port-au-Prince. There he was welcomed by a representative of the British government, and the retiring American minister, Ebenezer D. Bassett.

Despite his early worries about the climate, John found that Haiti was as gorgeous as it had been described: mountains, beautiful forests, limpid streams, flowers, fruits and vegetables, land and sea breezes. Its beauty and charm were just as he had read about when he was a boy. He observed that the sunsets were particularly stunning with their "indescribable radiance and glory, with the twilight lingering and playing about it often far till the evening" but the majestic mountains impressed him the most.

He was proud that he had been chosen to represent his country in such a place. The island seemed like the Garden of Eden. After touring, he decided he would live in Port-au-Prince, a tropical and handsome city overlooking the bay.

In the first few days, he made several trips into the city and was impressed by its wealth and culture. An official, whom he identifies only as General Lubin, was especially helpful offering the use of his horses, bridles, and saddles, the use of his library and help obtaining any information that John might need.

The capital city with a population of nearly 40,000, was easily accessible for all the Haitians, either by sea, foot, or horseback. Many businesses were located in fireproof buildings and the streets were well-drained. The port was busy. Island commerce included coffee, logwood, hides, honey, sugar, cotton and domestic animals. Fruit varieties included oranges, lemons, bananas, coconuts, and mangoes. John was surprised that, for unspecified reasons, the Haitians were not interested in cultivating their land, and efforts to get them to do so had failed.

The major parts of commerce and trade were in the hands of foreigners, such as the French, German, English or Americans.

As John learned more about the island, he was struck by local customs, such as how laundry was done. When he traveled from the country to the city, he saw women, scantily dressed, washing clothes in the streams. He described how they worked to Carrie before she and Frank visited. John said the women placed the clothes on a stone and beat them with a paddle, then used large amounts of soap to scrub them. The washers did not do ironing. That was done by women who were fully dressed.

Although John felt quite welcome, he knew he was at a disadvantage because he didn't speak French. Fortunately, he was able to communicate in English much of the time, and his helpful secretary, Adrian Lazare, spoke both French and Spanish. During one of Carrie and Frank's stays, the teen became proficient in the French language.

John was pleased that Frank had become a favorite of the islanders and Americans.

Shortly after his arrival, the Haitian president, Boirond-Canal, gave a reception for him and the retiring American minister. A full military band played in their honor. During the reception John noticed portraits of abolitionist John Brown and Senator Charles Sumner hanging on the wall. He told President Boirond-Canal that the senator was a special friend, who had urged him, in vain, to learn French. To John's surprise, the president left his seat, and in front of all the officials at the party, offered John his right hand and kissed him on the cheeks. "My government and people will treat the friend of Sumner with the kindest and most abiding consideration." With that, the band began playing the "famous John Brown song."

John learned that Haitians loved John Brown, particularly because he fought for freedom for slaves in the United States. And they loved Sumner because he had been a champion of black liberty in the States, and also because he had opposed the annexation of Santo Domingo by the United States. Haiti and the Dominican Republic share the island of Hispaniola.

As John settled into his duties, he realized that the location of the American Legation—where his office was situated—was not satisfactory. *A great government like ours should find quarters worthy of its character and its name,* he thought. He moved his offices into a building named *Sans*

Souci (without worry) in the central part of the city where other key government buildings were located.

On July 4, 1878, he hosted a party at his house for all members of the diplomatic and consular corps, and government officials, including the president and his cabinet. The dinner was deliberately American, but included local meat, fruit and vegetables.

After the holiday, he once again dealt with official business. Because of his background as an attorney, John was able to understand issues, such as trade, duties, and taxes involving the American shipping industry. In one instance five American ships had each been fined $50 for what was called a breach of law because their papers hadn't been properly certified by a Haitian consular officer in the port from which they had come. In fact, there were no such officers in those ports and the captains of the ships had done what was required under the circumstances—they had the papers notarized. John was able to resolve the situation.

John's subsequent detailed reports to Washington surprised officials because no one had ever sent them before from Haiti. He wrote that trade with Haiti could be expanded. But when American trade increased with the small island, it caused issues with other countries. Americans had introduced blue denim to the Haitians. On one occasion a German merchant, who had lost heavily on his investments in British goods, said to John, "The Haitians have gone crazy on American blue denims," to which John replied with a smile, "Their frenzy is the perfection of wisdom."

On the following Sunday, John was happy to see 16,000 members of the Haitian army parading—all dressed in pants and coats made of American blue denim.

In addition to working out trade issues, John helped resolve claims that Americans had filed against the Haitian government. His work involved diplomacy—listening to his fellow countrymen, while dealing with caution and care with the Haitians.

John M. Langston, professor at Howard University. (Courtesy of the Library of Congress.)

He also changed a tradition at the embassy. Prior to his arrival, Haitians involved in a revolution against the government had sought protection in the embassy. The past ambassadors and staff had sheltered them. John revoked that policy and declined to harbor political refugees. This helped discourage some revolutionary movements against the government, but uprisings continued as rebels conspired to oust President Boirond-Canal, who left the country before his term ended, hoping that would help save the country from further turmoil.

Not long after John arrived, there was an attempt to violently overthrow the government causing terror in the streets. John and other diplomats tried to prevent the threatened slaughter of prominent officials and the destruction of property. A bloody battle ensued and to John's dismay, some of the most beautiful buildings in Port-au-Prince were destroyed. Rebels also tried to kill his friend, General Lubin, while he and John were walking away from the national palace.

Guns were aimed; John convinced the rebels to not to fire, and the weapons were put away. The rebels sought refuge in various embassies, but not at the American one, and after they were detained, they were later shipped out of the country.

The turmoil created delicate situation for the foreigners and embassies in the country. But fortunately, the people elected General Louis Etienne Felicite Lysius Salomon, who had been in exile for many years, as their new president. Salomon had barely settled into the job, when a group plotted to overthrow him. After several months, the rebels gave up and surrendered their guns. They begged to be allowed to renew their allegiance to the government and live in peace. John helped work all this out, which restored peace and harmony, and triggered a great celebration.

President Salomon wrote a letter on December 30, 1883, thanking John for his service and added that he hoped he would remain in Haiti as long as possible.

An illustration from John's autobiography (page 392b) of a portrait of Haitian President General Louis Etienne Felicite Lysius Salomon with his autograph.

John's diplomatic duties did not end with the peace agreement. Several Americans living in Haiti had been harmed and their property destroyed during the revolution. They wanted to be compensated by the government. At first Haiti denied the claims, but John used his legal and diplomatic skills to help secure compensation for his fellow citizens.

He also assisted an American sea captain who was arrested and jailed on a charge of smuggling. John demanded the captain's release and the man was set free.

In addition to his eight years in Haiti, John served for two concurrent years as America's charge d'affaires in Santo Domingo.

The time in Haiti had other frightening moments for the family. During one of Carrie and Frank's long visits, Frank came down with smallpox. He might have died had it not been for the his mother's nursing care and her use of a burned sulphur disinfectant. On another occasion, when many foreigners came down with yellow fever, John was able to obtain tickets for Carrie and Frank to sail on an English ship leaving the island. John was not as fortunate, and he was stricken with yellow fever shortly after they sailed for home.

A few weeks later, Carrie received word that John had died from the disease. "We never should have left him," she said to her children. "If I had stayed to care for him, he wouldn't have died." His family was overjoyed to learn that the information was a mistake.

Finally, it was time to return to the States. John resigned his post as of January 31, 1885, when Democrat Grover Cleveland took office. However, he was asked to stay in Haiti until a replacement could be found. When his successor arrived, John introduced him to President Soloman and prepared to head for home.

His accomplishments as charge d'affaires—later called ambassador—were many. Haiti's Episcopal Bishop, James Theodore Holly, who had met

John years earlier in Cleveland, Ohio, reported on John's numerous successes during his tenure: John had assisted American seamen and shipwrecked sailors, helping them with clothing and housing. He helped the Haitian government in other ways, including in finance and law, and he had increased the number of American imports to the island. He also worked exporting more Haitian coffee to America. The bishop said John showed the highest form of patriotism and had endeavoured to have the diplomats from various countries work together.

Bishop Holly also noted that John was a great philanthropist, and advocated for self-governance. He said John had helped strengthen the idea that there should not be a single church supported by the state. The Roman Catholic Church should be on the same footing as all others.

The bishop concluded: "Mr. Langston . . . is so imbued with the spirit of American institutions and the genius of the America people . . . that a personal influence goes out from him . . . that is producing a salutary effect on the Haitian people and government. [The people] have found in him such a worthy, high-toned and faithful exponent of their liberty-loving principles, accredited to a struggling people that sadly need the aid of such wholesome examples in the perilous task that they have undertaken to carve out for themselves a high and noble destiny."

14

Called to New Service

THE ACCOLADES JOHN RECEIVED for his service in
Haiti meant nothing when it came to his
treatment upon his return to Washington. John had
not been compensated fully what he was owed by
his contract during time abroad. He was supposed
to receive $7,500 per year in gold, with no
allowance for all the extras he had to spend on
the job to entertain officials. He had paid for many
expenses out of his own pocket. To make matters
worse, while he was still in Haiti, Congressional
Democrats, through legal maneuvering, reduced
his salary to $5,000 per year. It was political
payback because of John's loyalty to the Republican
Party and its candidates.

While he was out of the country, he had no
choice but to accept the lower pay and deal with it
later. When he returned in July 1885, he demanded
that the government pay the balance of what he
was owed—$7,666.66. When he presented his bill
to the State Department, officials were surprised,

and questioned him about the legality of his demand. Eventually the State Department authorities agreed with John's legal claim and referred the matter to the Treasury Department, which disagreed and said he should be satisfied with what he had received.

John persisted, and found that George A. King, an established Washington attorney, was willing to take his unprecedented case to the Supreme Court. The lawsuit was successful, and the court ordered the government to pay John what he was owed plus interest. The victory was especially sweet as many in government and other attorneys predicted that John would lose.

Now it was time for John to take on new challenges. Not surprisingly, with his background in education and teaching, he was asked to be the president of Virginia Normal and Collegiate Institute, in Petersburg. (In 1946, the school changed its name to Virginia State University.) The college, which prepared students to become teachers, was founded in 1882 by General William Mahone's breakaway Readjuster Party, later Republican, as a reward to blacks for their support. One hundred twenty-six black students enrolled the first year on the thirty-three-acre campus with one building, a 200-book library, and a $20,000 budget.

While John was considering the offer, he received a letter on December 17, 1885, from the superintendent of education in the Commonwealth of Virginia that read: "In my judgment, if your duty ever called you to assume responsibilities the call is now made, and that if you want, an opportunity to serve your race and your country you now have it. . . . Come at once and take charge of the institution."

It was a dream come true. For years John considered returning to Virginia, perhaps even buying his father's former plantation and opening a school with high standards for black youths in Louisa County. He had attempted to purchase the property, but his offer was declined and he abandoned the plan. He agreed to accept the presidency as he felt it was his duty and an opportunity to lead.

John took a pay cut in order to accept the position. As president of this new college, he would receive just $1,500. However, he firmly believed that in his role he would be able to continue to help the emancipated classes of his native Virginia. He may also have seen his service as a step toward running for national office.

He was welcomed by officials, faculty and students and a large banquet was held in his honor. The Honorable A. W. Harris said in his toast that Langston "had come to Virginia to make, if possible, the institute the pride of Negroes in the country. He loved Virginia and would see her foremost again in the Union."

John began by reorganizing all branches of the fledgling institute to ensure that the best methods of instruction and wise discipline were in place. It seemed as though the entire school was

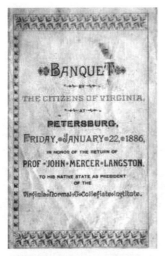

Front and inside pages from banquet program "in honor of the return of Professor John Mercer Langston to his native state and president of Virginia Normal and Collegiate Institute." (Courtesy of the Historically Black College and University Library Alliance, and Virginia State University archives.)

filled with a new vigor and determination. Under his leadership, the school's reputation improved rapidly and attendance increased.

To improve the school's morale, John personally led sessions on the teachings of Proverbs of Solomon, and worked with students on essays and orations. He and several instructors conducted required summer institutes for all teachers in black schools in the state.

Students and teachers excelled but there were, as usual, political worries. John had been appointed to the position of president of this state institution by a Republican administration, and now Democrats had been elected to key positions. John invited the new Democratic governor

171

Linda Salisbury

First Graduating Class, 1886

John Mercer Langston, president of Virginia Normal and Collegiate Institute, sits with the schools first graduating class. (Photo courtesy of Virginia State University Archives.)

Fitzhugh Lee, (also chairman of the State Board of Education), to visit the school and to listen to the students present essays and orations. Governor Lee did attend, along with other state officials. John said this was the first time in the state of Virginia that a governor had honored a black college with his presence. The first small senior class—eight students—was graduated in 1886. In 1887, the graduating class invited the governor to attend graduation services and asked him to hand out the diplomas and address the students. Governor Lee not only participated as asked, but also stayed the rest of the day. When the governor

172

spoke with state lawmakers later, he noted the increase in enrollment and said that the school was in "good condition." He also said that the work of the school had been hampered by the "want of accommodations." A new building completed in January 1888 accommodated 700 students.

John was frustrated by having to answer to two state boards—the Board of Visitors (Democrats) and the State Board of Education (black members). He felt the dual boards created conflicts in how to manage the school. John was caught in the untenable political strife between the parties. Despite the devotion of students and their parents, he decided to resign at the end of 1887. His lifelong support of the Republican Party had caused friction with the Democrats, who would not have renewed his contract. He was ultimately left without authority and control. A loyal Republican, he would not switch parties just to save his job. Not even a high compliment given him by a member of the Board of Visitors could entice him to stay. The man declared, "You have conducted this school in such a manner that we cannot now take up a newspaper of the State without finding some allusion to it with complimentary mention of its work and accomplishments. It is even placed beside the state university itself."

John knew that "That was a substantial and remarkable commendation of his work."

He announced his decision to the faculty and students during the 1887 Christmas holiday. The students gave him a "golden shield, significant in its form, unique in its beauty and rare in its richness, bearing on either side in engraved characters and figures words and designs of tenderness and honor."

The students also prepared a proclamation that included these words: "That we most cordially thank him not only as our president, but as the educator of the race for his unequalled utterances upon all questions pertaining to their welfare, making himself the champion of their cause."

There were numerous speeches at John's farewell, and then a student, Charles Seales, who had presented the shield, said, "You have taught us to look up to you not only as a wise instructor but as a guardian and friend . . . and when we go into the world [we] shall remember you with filial regard as champion and prince of our cause."

It was an emotional time for John. He was attached to his students and stayed in touch with many of them as they went on to further studies in medicine and law at such schools as Harvard and Amherst. John appreciated the assistance that whites gave them so that they could pay for their expenses at these schools where they met with great success.

15

The Sword and the Broom

THE FINAL PHASE OF HIS PUBLIC LIFE was the most political yet and also the most frustrating. On December 31, 1887, John was headed to speak in Salem, Virginia, at a Great Emancipation celebration. When the train stopped briefly in Farmville, the county seat of Prince Edward County, he had a surprise visit. A committee asked him if he would meet with them when he returned two days later. Farmville was one of the most populated areas in the Fourth Congressional District, and politically important for the Republican party.

The meeting, held in the house of a distinguished black community leader, was attended by both white and black Republicans from Prince Edward and neighboring counties of Lunenburg, Powhatan and Nottoway. They had heard that John planned to leave the state after his resignation from Virginia Normal and Collegiate Institute; the group wanted to convince John that he should be a candidate for Congress instead. They said he owed it to the people of his district, and especially blacks in the state and the nation to do so. The Republicans were the majority in the district, so those at the meeting were certain that John could not only be nominated, but also could win.

John listened carefully to their proposal. He said that before he could make a decision he needed to talk with friends who lived in other parts of the district. Soon he decided to run.

He first canvassed the district to see how voters felt, then formally announced his candidacy. His advisors suggested that he first run as a delegate to the Republican national convention in Chicago the following June when the president and vice president would be nominated. John campaigned tirelessly around his district for the position of delegate. He made speeches to all classes of people and from various political parties, talking about Republican principles and measures. He spoke at courthouses in every county and in towns and homes. When the audiences were too large for a hall, he spoke to them outside.

He would soon find out how nasty politics could become. The race for the congressional seat—ultimately with three candidates—was complicated and bitter. When John returned to Petersburg from the national convention in July, he discovered that in his absence, General William Mahone, who ran the Republican Party "machine" in the district, was launching a dirty campaign against him. Mahone issued a proclamation, supported by his followers,

Former Confederate General William Mahone, who was commander at the battle of the Crater in Petersburg in 1865, during which he led the charge to massacre black Union troops. He was a railroad man, a former slave owner and politician.

that "no colored man would be allowed" to represent the Fourth Congressional District of Virginia in the Congress of the United States.

Mahone held a conference at his house on July 31 to lay out his devious plans for defeating John, if he should succeed in being nominated. John knew that Mahone, who was enlisting the help of Democrats, would use any trick or method he could at the polls to commit fraud. That included miscounting or discarding ballots. They would use fraud and bribery—anything they could think of to keep John's supporters from voting—because he was "colored." All John's achievements, all of his appointments and experience meant nothing to Mahone and his corrupt followers.

At least one honorable Democrat would not support Mahone, and commented, "Are we dogs that we should do this thing?"

Linda Salisbury

The September convention to nominate a candidate for Congress split the Republican Party. When Mahone's group announced that by a credentials canvass, John would receive only thirty-three of the eighty-five delegates, John's supporters left the hall, with a bugler leading the way, and held their own convention. They nominated John as the Independent Republican candidate.

John addressed the Independent Republicans convention and assured delegates that he would be an honorable and devoted Republican and defend party principles. He would dignify the name of his district and state. His speech was met

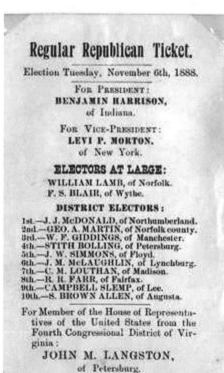

An 1888 election poster showing the Republican ticket, including John Mercer Langston of Petersburg, who was running for a seat in Congress. (Courtesy of the Historically Black College and University Library Alliance and Virginia State University Archives.)

with great applause. When he returned to Petersburg, his fellow citizens made him ride in a carriage drawn by four white horses and decorated with United States flags. The parade went through the major streets of the city and ended at his campaign headquarters dubbed "Langston Hall," where thousands were waiting to hear him. They sang and cheered. John spoke for forty-five minutes, saying that he was "in rebellion against tyranny," and "an upholder of the dignity of my race."

The Fourth Congressional District was comprised of eleven counties. Its population consisted of former slave owners, and a large population of freed slaves. This area was called the "Black Belt of Virginia" because during redistricting by the Democrats, it now contained more blacks than whites. The city of Petersburg had a similar population mix. Although black residents outnumbered whites, those black voters had been under the control of an established politician, General Mahone, who claimed that he could do more for them than anyone, including John. Could John win them over? The Republican party was now divided between Mahone's candidate as a "regular" Republican, and John's candidacy as an Independent Republican. Most white Republican voters would not support John. He also faced considerable opposition from the Democrats, who controlled voter registration, judgeships and clerkships.

There was much to overcome if he were to be elected. As a delegate to the national convention, he was sure he could count on the support of black voters and women of the district. Even though women couldn't vote, they pledged to help in whatever way they could.

John was also aware that Mahone would make every effort to secure support of the National Republican Committee, and that he might be given large amounts of money for the campaign.

Despite the obstacles, John had faith in the voters. He continued to make speeches and organized clubs to support his candidacy. Men and women printed and distributed campaign materials. He put together a general committee of blacks and whites. Once the committee was established in its headquarters in Petersburg, members took a communication from John to Mahone advising him that a large number of Republicans supported John's candidacy rather than Mahone's choice. Mahone continued to call John a "bolter" from the party, who was only running for his own "selfish ends." Venable refused to debate him.

Support for John, as an Independent Republican, grew across the district and political clubs—called the Invincibles—were organized for men, and women.

John observed that "the women could and did exert large influence in controlling and directing the men in their political purposes and conduct."

He realized that his "success in the district was more entirely due to the influence of women than to any other single cause."

He made his official speeches as a candidate, and although he was well received, he was warned that it might not be safe to attend meetings in several parts of the district. He ignored the warnings and was only interrupted a few times by "ruffany" black men hired by General Mahone to cause trouble. In the first case, the troublemaker was soon stopped by "respectable whites and blacks."

On another occasion, threats were made in an effort to keep John from speaking at a meeting, but he arrived anyway and was "received with demonstrations of enthusiastic deafening applause" by the 5,000 gathered. When he was again interrupted, he warned the heckler to stop and the audience applauded him.

Although Mahone and his followers were trying everything they could to keep John from running and winning, he had much popular support. He knew that his candidacy was based on his outstanding qualifications, which made his enemies fear his potential influence in Congress.

As the campaign heated up, Mahone and his followers decided to enlist the help of black men living outside the borders of Virginia to discredit John's reputation. John's longtime rival, Frederick Douglass, was one of them. Mahone hoped that the outsiders' attacks would sway voters. In a letter, Douglass accused John of having "mad political ambition" and said that he had only stayed around Howard University until it was clear that he wouldn't be president. He implied that John was at fault for the banking problems at the Freedman's Bank.

There was a swift backlash from black newspapers against this personal attack. John said Douglass had offered a "cunning, false and base testimony" against him, and was filled with "poor logic, irrelevant philosophy, and false, malicious assertions."

Frederick Douglass, orator, self-educated fugitive slave, abolitionist, advocate for women's rights, a journalist, diplomat to Haiti, authored three auto-biographies. He and John knew each other, but while respecting each other's skills, were rivals. Douglass' opposition to John's candidacy was personal and nasty and backfired in black newspapers.

(Courtesy National Archives.)

John countered the letter's claims with statements of support from church leaders, including Bishop James T. Holly, of Haiti, a former U.S. resident. In his testimony, the bishop called it almost treasonous for a black man to oppose John's election in light of his outstanding qualifications. John's record of fighting for black citizens before and after the Civil War was well known.

Instead of working against John, the Douglass letter had the opposite effect. It was not the first time these nationally known rivals had clashed.

In 1884, when John's youngest son, Frank, had been charged with but acquitted of murder, Douglass had made insensitive remarks about Frank, which only deepened their division.

John understood the importance of the election of 1888. He felt the party that had saved the Union, the party of Lincoln, should be in control. Republicans were divided in the Fourth Congressional District and the Democrats hoped to take advantage of that. John knew that conspiracy was in the works from his opponents in both parties. He didn't doubt the support of voters, but he was concerned about tricks and fraud at the polls on election day. He and his supporters knew they needed to watch and document what went on in the more than 100 precincts. John made sure that 500 of his workers each had a blank book, an envelope and a set of instructions for election day documentation. Voters were asked to report loudly to his pollwatchers whether they had been able to vote or were denied. The volunteers made notes. This way John would know what the final count should be. His opponents were the Democrat E. C. Venable and Mahone's unimpressive Republican candidate, Judge R. W. Arnold. The election results were rigged as expected.

By the time John had voted, he had learned that many black voters holding ballots printed with his name, had already been blocked from casting ballots. "This condition was caused by the unheard of and unjustifiable arrangement whereby two lines had been set up for voters coming to the polls." One line was for white persons, Democrats and Republicans, and another line for black Republican voters. If John himself had not been moved to the front of the line for black Republicans, he said he would have been in line for three hours to make his way to the window where he would cast his ballot. Black voters were discouraged by the long wait, and at day's end, many in the district had gone home without casting ballots. The long lines were just one way that Mahone and Democrats tampered with the results.

John and his supporters decided to take names of these voters and where they lived, and write in John's name, in front of clerks hired by John, on the back of the ballots. The ballots were sealed and guarded, then taken to the Committee on Contested Election Cases. It looked as if the winner was the Democrat, Venable, with 13,298 votes, with John next with 12,657, and Republican Arnold trailing with 3,207. Venable was seated.

John was exhausted, but not done. He would fight the fraudulent election results. He tried to hire several attorneys in Petersburg to work with him, but they declined, saying that they feared social retribution by his Republican opposition. "Mahone would never forgive me," said one.

John wondered, *Would the enemies of justice and right, through their selfish social influences, finally shipwreck the honest ballot of a loyal constituency?*

Eventually, John hired three young black attorneys with no local affiliations. They weren't worried about threats or rejection in Petersburg. Their task was to take testimony from witnesses. Venable's attorneys were doing the same and trying to cast doubt on the credibility of witnesses for John, again through dirty tricks.

Frank N. Robinson was called as a witness about the fraud at noon on January 31, 1889, and was asked eight questions by John's attorneys. Venable's attorneys, and even Venable, cross-examined the man with 316 questions, a session that lasted until February 6. John said most of the questions had nothing to do with the election. And when the poor witness was finished, he was arrested on a complaint that he had not testified in the case.

Finally, the materials were presented to the Congressional Committee on Contested Elections, which favored John in its decision on May 23, 1890, nineteen months after the election. John credited N. P. Hagen, a representative from Wisconsin, who chaired a subcommittee on the case, for understanding the full truth of what had gone on and for supporting his claim.

Fierce opposition was still working against him. Democrats notified Republicans in Congress that they would never agree to seating John.

On September 23, 1890, after more delays, Congress adopted two resolutions, one that removed Venable from his seat, and the second resolving that John was entitled be seated. John was sworn in and took his seat in the House of Representatives to "enthusiastic Republican approval and applause." Only the Republicans were clapping. Every Democrat in the House walked out while John was taking the oath of office. It was a "foul and malicious spirit," he said.

In a strange turn of events, after John was seated, instead of leaving for the day, the Democrats returned and many congratulated him on his success.

On the following day, when he entered the House, John found his seat covered with flowers from well-wishers. One floral arrangement had special significance. Its design included a sword representing overcoming his opposition, and the broom of destruction "with which Good Providence had swept them out of his pathway to victory."

Illustration on page 498a of John's autobiography titled "Admission into the House of Representatives, September 23, 1890. Note all the empty seats on the Democratic side of the aisle.

Because of the delay had lasted most of his term in Congress, by the time John began to serve in the House of Representatives, he had to start all over and run for re-election. He lost the 1890 contest to Democrat James Fletcher Epes, 9,991 to 13,325, who would hold the seat in the 52nd and 53rd Congresses. Disheartened, John decided not to challenge these results, despite suspicion of more fraud and intimidation that cost him the election again.

Still, he tried to use his shortened term to do some good. Congress was not in session during parts of the fall. During that time, John visited his district and also sat on the Committee of Education. The final three months of his term began December 1, 1890. One of his first proposals was to reimburse customers of the Freedman's Bank. He also proposed a national literacy test for voters in federal elections, and a national trade or industrial school for blacks. He proposed a resolution to amend the Constitution in regards to national voting rights and the manner of electing presidential electors representatives and senators. One requirement would be that voters should be able to read and write in English. (He did not include the right of women to vote although he and Charles had argued for women's suffrage.) He proposed a bill to observe February 12 and April 27 as national holidays in memory, and honor, of Lincoln and Grant and he tried to let blacks be admitted to national military schools

He assisted the Republican majority by voting in favor of the controversial McKinley Tariff, which drove up the price of inexpensive goods manufactured abroad. A Democratic newspaper accused him of building a wall "so high and so great that the British lion would never have been able to get over it without the aid of dynamite or a scaling ladder."

Sadly, none of his bills he proposed passed. There had been much he had wanted to accomplish but success slipped away because he had to fight

Illustration from John's autobiography (page 515a) titled "Making his first speech in the House of Representatives, January 16, 1891.")

so long for his seat and had little time to build the political relationships among fellow representatives that are necessary to gain support for legislation.

He made two speeches on the floor of Congress, one was on the merchant marines, and the other, on January 16, 1891, supported the "Force Bill" that the Senate had refused to consider. The bill would have provided for supervision of federal elections to guarantee blacks fair treatment when they voted.

His addresses to Congress, again, showcased his skills as an orator. The Cleveland *Leader* on January 17, 1891, reported that his memorable speech "brings moisture to the eyes of hardened old Bourbon members."

During his time in Congress, John was treated with kindness by the president and cabinet members, and was successful having applicants from his district find service government jobs.

He chose not to use his "sword and broom" to once again take on Mahone's machine (Mahone was now governor) in a re-election bid after Epes' first term. Mahone accused John of dividing the electorate through racism and called him "almost a Democrat." In 1892, he became the Republican Party nominee, but declined to run. John knew the ballots would once more be dishonestly and mischievously manipulated. He had served in Congress, but he was done.

He was sixty-four years of age.

16

Final Years

IN "RETIREMENT" from his exhausting, short but ultimately triumphant political career, John was able to turn greater attention to his family and home he enjoyed near the campus of Howard University. After leaving Oberlin in 1871, he had built and moved to the unique Swiss-cottage-style of Hillside Cottage. From his windows he was able to see the Capitol. The three-story house (one floor was the basement) on the corner of Fourth and College streets had fourteen rooms and was across from a large public park.

The acres surrounding the house at 2225 Fourth Street NW had room for a barn, hennery and stable. John enjoyed his property's natural and ornamental trees, including a magnolia from France given to the family by a friend, twenty-two years earlier, when the house was built. Massachusetts Senator Charles Sumner had provided several trees, including a classic sycamore, and there were also numerous fruit trees on his property. John could look at the trees and remember working with the senator on drafting the Civil Rights Act of 1875. Here John could rest, spend time with his family, practice law, and reflect on his life and careers as he contemplated writing his autobiography. He also served as a trustee on the new St. Paul's Normal and Industrial School in Lawrenceville, Virginia.

He thought about his children, their first daughter, Chinque, who had died as a toddler and was buried at Oberlin. The other four children were now grown and healthy.

Illustration on page 520b of John's autobiography shows Hillside Cottage in Washington, D.C.

Their son, Arthur, completed his education at Oberlin and taught in black public schools in St. Louis, Missouri, until he was promoted to principal of the large Dessalines school. He had married the musically talented Ida Napier, who was trained at Fisk University and also Oberlin. The couple had two "splendid" boys, the elder named for John, and the other named after his mother's brother, James Carroll. John was a proud grandfather. Ralph also went to Oberlin, then trained in business at a commercial college and took a job in the Government Printing Office in Washington. He married Anna Pearl Jackson, an accomplished musician. The couple moved to Nashville, Tennessee, where he had a furniture business, then later returned to Washington.

John adored little Nettie Matilde Langston, Ralph and Anna's only child. "Bright, yet docile and well-behaved, she is, so far as her grandparents are concerned, on both sides, the object of their delight and satisfaction," he wrote.

John and Carrie's daughter, Nettie, married James C. Napier, the brother of Arthur's wife. They had no children of their own and were very involved with Arthur and Ida's boys. Nettie was involved with church and educational matters and enjoyed singing. The couple often visited her parents at Hillside Cottage.

Then there was Frank, the youngest. He, too, spent time at Oberlin, and also in West Newton, Massachusetts. John loved Frank's remarkable spirit, and felt his nickname of Lamb (given by his brothers and sister) was appropriate. John doesn't mention this in his narrative, but Frank was arrested and later acquitted on a murder charge when he foolishly fired in the vicinity of a crowd and one of the bullets caused a fatality.

After the Langstons had returned home from Haiti, Frank was hired by the Government Printing Office and learned to be a bookbinder. Later, with John's assistance, he opened a book and stationary business in Petersburg. He later married India Watkins of Town Creek, Alabama. They named their daughter Carrie Cornelia for her grandmothers.

From his chair on the shady porch, John reflected on how fortunate he was to have married Carrie. She had been an excellent mother, raising the children with discipline but without scolding or severe bodily punishment. He thought, *Today there is not one among them who does not affectionately honor, praise and bless her, and not one who does not deem himself happy in her association and companionship.* Carrie had always been a sympathizing companion for him in every aspect of his private and public life. They were united in their views and political and religious convictions.

John felt peace at the deepening shadows and mused further. He was also thankful for their many friends around the country and enjoyed spending time in Petersburg where he also had a residence. But Washington had become their home, where he had large and valuable library of rare books that he had collected for more than fifty years. Proclamations and bestowed honors decorated his walls. He and Carrie were in good health, and were blessed with a life that had given them name, standing and honor in the country. It had been quite a journey for the orphan from a Virginia plantation. He could be justifiably proud of his achievements for his race, family and nation, despite ugly politics.

Further inspired to write, he returned to his library, leaned forward in his leather chair and removed a blank piece of paper from a tray and dipped his pen in the inkwell. As he completed his book he wrote, "Of all the persons who in 1834 left the old Virginia plantation for Ohio, the child of the company, now an old man is the only survivor. And he is delighted that he may make just mention in these reminiscences of his relatives and friends composing that company, all of whom have gone to their long, deep sleep!"

His 534-page autobiography, *From the Virginia Plantation to the National Capitol*, was published in 1894 by the American Publishing Company, Hartford, Connecticut.

On the first anniversary of Oklahoma statehood, April 22, 1890, Langston City was officially established, and later Langston University, also named for him because of his contributions to education and public affairs. In his later years John continued to speak on issues of race and equality. He died on November 15, 1897, from acute indigestion, mostly like a heart attack, at Hillside Cottage, and was buried in Woodlawn Cemetery in Washington, D.C.

The Rest of the Family

John Mercer Langston does not mention these family members during his autobiography's conclusion, however, their lives are also worth nothing.

Maria Powell remained in Louisa County with her slave-husband, Joseph; the couple had twenty-one children. At her death in 1850, she willed Joseph to their son, Albert. It's possible that the foundation of a house found near the graves of her parents at the Powell corner of the Quarles plantation, in the vicinity of Kent's Mill, was Maria's home.

Gideon Quarles Langston: Was born in 1815 and died in 1861. In 1844, he married Ann Clark, the sister of one of John's lifelong friends, Peter Clark. John had met the Clarks while boarding with the Woodson family in Cincinnati.

Charles Henry Langston: Charles gained prominence as a fearless and outspoken abolitionist, active with John in the Ohio Antislavery movement, eloquent orator and teacher. He moved to

Kansas during the Civil War and was a leader in
the state campaign from 1863 to 1867 for black
voting rights. Charles lobbied Samuel Crawford,
Radical Republican nominee for governor, to propose a referendum to eliminate the word "white"
from state voting qualifications. The referendum
was defeated, but in 1870, blacks received the right
to vote with the passage of the 15th Amendment.
Charles was appointed as the Freedmen's Bureau's
general superintendent in Kansas. In 1872, he was
named principal of the Quindaro Freedman's
School (later Western University), the first black
college west of the Mississippi. Charles helped
raise black troops during the Civil War and later
founded the Interstate Library Association.

After his first wife died, Charles married Mary
Patterson Leary, whose husband was killed during John Brown's raid at Harper's Ferry after being recruited by John in Oberlin. Mary's daughter, Louise, was from her first marriage. She and
Charles had two children together, Nathaniel
Turner Langston, named for the leader of a slave
rebellion in Virginia; and Caroline Mercer Langston, named for John's wife, Carrie. The Langstons
lived in Lawrence, Kansas, for the rest of their
lives. Their daughter, Caroline, married James N.
Hughes and had a son, (John Mercer) Langston
Hughes, the famed American poet. The Langstons
also had a foster son, named Dessalines.

Charles Henry Langston died in 1892.

Acknowledgments

I'M EVER GRATEFUL to those who have provided encouragement, thoughtful questions, suggestions, and proofreading assistance: My husband, Jim, who designed the sword and broom graphic and for his excellent ideas. Special thanks to Abigail Grotke; Elizabeth Madden; Reed Browning; Julie Franklin; Shanna Hart; and Mary-Frances Hoh. And to the ever-helpful Ken Grossi, Oberlin College archivist; members of historical societies and digital archives, including Elaine Taylor, executive director of the Louisa County, Virginia's, Sargeant Museum; Marcia DePalma, Brownhelm, Ohio, Historical Society; Francine Archer, Virginia State University archivist; Robert Harvey, railroad historian; Pattie Cooke, Louisa historian; Gordonsville Exchange Hotel and Civil War Museum; also to the Library of Congress reference department; Howard University; and Helene and Jerl Purcell for a tour of Ralph Quarles plantation home.

Resources

I have used many more resources than the ones listed below, but these are significant references that I recommend. Please read on-line or in print:

1. *From the Virginia Plantation to the National Capital* by John Mercer Langston. It is out of copyright so there are several print additions. (Old South Books is the one I purchased.)

2. *John Mercer Langston and the Fight for Black Freedom, 1829–65* by William Cheek and Aimee Cheek (University of Illinois Press). Detailed, scholarly and illuminating. I drew from it for personal details, such as how Langston and Carrie addressed each other, and her college background.

3. *Narrative of the Life of Frederick Douglass, an American Slave (1845)*. Douglass' account of his life, born of a white man and a slave mother, whom he never really knew, his self-education and abuse by various slave owners in Maryland, is heart-wrenching and inspiring, and reveals the contrast of his early years with Langston's.

4. "A Negro Runs for Congress: John Mercer Langston and the Virginia Campaign of 1888," a 1965 article by William Cheek, published by The Association for the Study of African American Life and History Vol. 52, No 1 (January 1967) (Library of Congress. Cheek's concluding remarks help explain why Langston's name is not been well known even in Virginia history.

5. Oberlin College Archives for speeches by John Mercer Langston and an account of the Oberlin-Wellington raid. You will see how he hammers at the Constitutional and legal reasons against slavery and voting rights.

6. "The Oberlin Fugitive Slave Rescue: A Victory of Higher Law," by Steven Lubet, Northwestern School of Law Scholarly Commons Faculty Working Papers. An excellent account.

7. "Oration in Memory of Abraham Lincoln," Frederick Douglass, TeachingAmericanHistory.org.

8. "John Mercer Langston (1829–1897)," encyclopediavirginia.org

9. "Buried Truth: John Mercer Langston: A trailblazer in Virginia politics," by Zann Nelson, March 18, 2016, www.dailyprogress.com

10. *The "Colored Hero" of Harper's Ferry, John Anthony Copeland and the War against Slavery,* Seven Lubet. (2015, Cambridge University Press) A fascinating history of Copeland, one of the Oberlin Rescurers, and Charles Henry Langston's role in the antislavery activities.

11. "Charles Henry Langston and the African American Struggle in Kansas," Richard B. Sheridan, www.ksh.org. Winter 1999 publication.

Index

Buchanan, James, 93
Burke, Edmund, 145
Bushnell, Simeon, 92, 94–95
"bushwhackers," 107

C
Calhoun, John C., 66–67
Chase, Salmon P., 115–116
Cheek, William, 9
civil rights, 5, 108–109, 191
Civil Rights Act, 191
Civil Rights bill, 5
Civil War, 97–98, 104, 106–109
Clark, Ann, 195
Clark, Peter, 195
Cleveland, Grover, 166
Colburn, Annie, 36–38
Colored Troops regiment, 100–102, 105. *See also* troops, recruiting
Congressional race, 175–189
Constitution, 5, 8, 84, 105, 108–109, 141–142, 187
Cooke, H. D., 149
Copeland, John Anthony, Jr., 93, 97
Cowles, Henry, 71
Cox, Christopher C., 148–149
Cox, Samuel, 59
Crawford, Samuel, 195
Custer, George, 128
Cuthbert, William, 53

D
Declaration of Independence, 8, 84
Dessalines, Jean-Jacques, 158
Deveaux, Samuel, 60–61
Dewey, Major, 104
discrimination, 62–63, 123–125. *See also* prejudice
Douglass, Frederick, 6, 8–9, 153–156, 181–183
Downey, William, 122
Dred Scott case, 90
Dudley, L. Edwin, 123, 139
Dunn, Oscar J., 142

Linda Salisbury

E
election fraud, 183–187
emancipation, 106–109
Emancipation Proclamation, 97, 98
Emancipation statue, 152–154
Emerson, Ralph Waldo, 144–146
Epes, James Fletcher, 187, 189
Exchange Hotel, 125–126

F
Fairchild, Charles, 82
Fairchild, James H., 82, 92
Farnsworth, General, 122, 123
Fifteenth Amendment, 141
Finney, Charles Grandison, 56, 71–72
Fitch, James, 92
Fourteenth Amendment, 141
Fowler, John, 66–69
free blacks, 25–26, 107, 133
freed slaves, 26, 106–109, 120, 152, 179
Freedman's Bank, 154, 182, 187
Freedmen's Bureau, 6, 117–122, 125–126, 138, 140, 143, 196
From the Virginia Plantation to the National Capitol, 6, 194
Fugitive Slave Act, 26, 90, 94–95, 113
fugitive slaves
    "ghosts" as, 13–17, 90, 104
    helping, 26, 46, 54–55, 90–95, 118
    slave-catchers and, 26, 90–92

G
Garrison, William Lloyd, 83
"ghosts," 13–17, 90, 104. *See also* fugitive slaves
Goethe, Johann Wolfgang von, 145
Gooch, Matilda, 32–33
Gooch, Virginia, 33–36, 51, 56
Gooch, William, 21, 28, 32–43, 50–51, 133
Gooch family, 7, 30–44, 50–52
Gordon, William Fitzhugh, Jr., 130, 133–136
government pay, 168–169
Grant, Ulysses S., 104, 114, 139–140, 144–145, 148, 153

H
Hagen, N. P., 185
Haitian appointment, 157–167
Harper's Ferry, 93, 96–97, 196
Harris, A. W., 170
Hayes, Rutherford B., 157
health board, 148–152
Hickman, Wade, 105
Holly, James Theodore, 166–167, 182
Howard, Oliver Otis, 117, 119–121, 138–139, 143, 146–147
Howard University, 5–6, 119, 143–145, 151–152, 181, 190
Hughes, James N., 196
Hughes, Langston, 9, 196

J
Jackson, Anna Pearl, 192
Jackson, John, 59
Johnson, Andrew, 102, 105, 112–115, 138–139
Johnson, John T., 139

K
Kent, William, 136–137
Kent's Mill, 13, 129, 137, 195
King, George A., 169

L
Langston, Ann Clark, 195
Langston, Anna Pearl Jackson, 192
Langston, Arthur Dessalines, 86, 89, 107, 191
Langston, Caroline "Carrie," 6–7, 80–86, 89–90, 100, 107–108, 119, 160, 166, 193, 196
Langston, Caroline Mercer, 196
Langston, Carrie Cornelia, 193
Langston, Charles, 11, 14–19, 24, 28–32, 52–53, 58–62, 86, 91–97, 195–196
Langston, Chinque, 90, 191
Langston, Dessalines, 196
Langston, Frank, 90, 107, 160–161, 166, 183, 192–193
Langston, Gideon, 11, 16–19, 24, 27–32, 45, 48–49, 52–53, 195
Langston, Harriet, 15, 30
Langston, Ida Napier, 191
Langston, India Watkins, 193
Langston, James Carroll, 192

Linda Salisbury

LINDA SALISBURY, an Oberlin College graduate with a degree in English, retired to Virginia after a career in journalism. She has written extensively about Louisa County, Virginia, its people and its history, in both her children's series and free-lance articles. She's the author of eighteen books for children and adults.